W9-AGG-014

SIX TRAITS

FOR WRITING

Middle School

HOLT, RINEHART AND WINSTON

Copyright © Holt, Rinehart and Winston

All rights reserved. No part of this publication may be reproduced or transmitted in any form or by any means, electronic or mechanical, including photocopy, recording, or any information storage and retrieval system, without permission in writing from the publisher.

Teachers may photocopy pages in sufficient quantity for classroom use only, not for resale.

Printed in the United States of America

If you have received these materials as examination copies free of charge, Holt, Rinehart and Winston retains title to the materials and they may not be resold. Resale of examination copies is strictly prohibited.

Possession of this publication in print format does not entitle users to convert this publication, or any portion of it, into electronic format.

2 3 4 5   1689   12 11 10 09

TABLE OF CONTENTS

Copyright © 2007 by Holt, Rinehart and Winston. All rights reserved.

Six Traits: Worksheets:

Copyright © 2007 by Holt, Rinehart and Winston. All rights reserved.

INTRODUCTION

To the Teacher

In the mid-1980s, a group of seventeen teachers in Oregon formed the Analytical Writing Assessment Committee. Their goal was to create a logical rubric to help teachers evaluate their students' writing in a consistent and fair way. They identified six key elements that should appear in every piece of student writing and developed scoring guides for each one. The result was the six-traits rubrics.

What Are the Six Traits and the Six-Trait Rubrics?

The six traits are elements of writing that your students already know and use. Specifically, they are **1) ideas and content, 2) organization, 3) voice, 4) word choice, 5) sentence fluency,** and **6) conventions.** The rubrics provide a consistent vocabulary and a clear set of criteria for evaluating each trait on a scale of 5–3–1. The rubrics identify the benchmarks of excellent, adequate, and poor writing for each trait. Teachers and students may use the rubrics to get an overview of how well a paper articulates ideas and expresses a point of view, voice, and style.

How do the Six Traits Help Me Evaluate My Students' Work?

The six-traits rubrics help you focus when you read and evaluate your students' papers. By providing you with a consistent vocabulary for discussing and thinking about writing and by offering you a standard set of criteria, you can evaluate a paper quickly and accurately. The ideas contained in the rubrics are not new. Nor are they yet another "angle" or writing "fad." They are concepts that you have already taught your students. The rubrics help you evaluate how your student is writing at a particular point in time, for a particular writing assignment.

How Do the Six Traits Help My Students?

The six traits put your students in control of their own writing. The rubrics offer them a clear, understandable language and a logical set of criteria for evaluating different aspects of their work. The rubrics break down the process of self-evaluation into six steps. By focusing on one trait at a time as they review their own or another person's writing, students can get a sense of their strengths and weaknesses. They can reach an authentic assessment of where the writer stands with *that* piece of writing at *that* point in his or her development as a writer. In other words, the rubrics provide not a score or a grade, but a balanced overview of how students use six key elements in their writing. For example, after writing a draft of a persuasive essay, a student can use the six-traits rubrics to discover that her ideas and organization are strong but that her voice and word choice are a little weak, her sentences tend to run on, and she really needs to review the rules for using commas. She can use the specific criteria in the rubrics to pinpoint the areas that need "polish."

Copyright © 2007 by Holt, Rinehart and Winston. All rights reserved.

How Do the Six-Traits Rubrics "Fit" with the Writing Process?

Student writers can integrate the rubrics at each step in the writing process—not just when they revise their work. For example, in the prewriting stage, writers focus on ideas and content and begin thinking about organizational strategies. In the writing stage, they focus more on content, organization, and voice. As they revise and edit their drafts, they make sure that their ideas and organizational strategies are sound, their voice and word choice are appropriate, and their sentences add structure, rhythm, and style to their writing. As they proofread, they concentrate on their sentence structures and their implementation of writing conventions. Good writers already synthesize ideas, organization, voice, word choice, sentence structure, and conventions as they prepare their papers. The six- traits rubrics help students at every level examine these elements and see how they integrate in their writing.

How Do I Use This Book?

PART ONE of this book provides you and your students with an overview and explanation of the six traits. Part One also contains student-written essays (expository, persuasive, and narrative) and evaluations of those essays based on the six-traits rubrics. Our goal is to show students how they can use the six traits to evaluate another person's writing. In addition, Part One contains three student essays that students can evaluate on their own. They can practice applying the rubrics to another person's writing.

PART TWO shows students how to use the six traits at each stage of the writing process. It contains three mini writing workshops (expository, persuasive, and narrative) that guide students through the process of writing while considering the six traits.

PART THREE provides a review of how to read and analyze a writing prompt, followed by eighteen writing prompts. The prompts are similar to those found on many state-mandated tests. They challenge students to write in three different modes—expository, persuasive, and narrative writing— and at different levels of difficulty.

PART FOUR contains rubrics, worksheets, and other support materials that help students use the rubrics and refine their own writing skills. In Part Four, you will find six-traits rubrics for both teachers and students. Flashcards will help students become acquainted with the level 5 rubric for each of the six traits. A blank evaluation form appears in Part Four, as well. In addition, Part Four contains nearly two dozen trait-specific worksheets to help students at each stage of the writing process.

Copyright © 2007 by Holt, Rinehart and Winston. All rights reserved.

PART ONE

USING THE SIX TRAITS TO
EVALUATE STUDENT WRITING

IDEAS AND CONTENT

Ideas and content are the most important parts of any paper. They are the paper's message—its theme, main idea, or story line. A paper without ideas is like a house built on swampy land. Without firm ground to support it, it will wobble and fall. A paper with a firm foundation of good ideas will, like a soaring skyscraper or majestic castle, make people pay attention and show them something interesting.

Before you can determine if a paper has good ideas and content, you may want to review the following terms: **main idea, details, purpose,** and **audience.** These elements contribute to ideas and content.

Main idea	A **main idea** is the most important point in a piece of writing. It may be stated directly, but sometimes a writer will hint at the main idea by dropping clues. That is an implied main idea.
Details	**Details** are the supporting ideas that help a writer flesh out an idea. Details might take the form of evidence in a persuasive paper—facts, statistics, examples, and anecdotes—that help the writer to convince readers to think or do something. In a narrative or expository paper, details help readers imagine a new idea or a particular event.
Purpose	The **writer's purpose** is the reason he or she is writing. The writer might want to share information, express feelings, or influence the way others think or act.
Audience	Writer's pay attention to their **audience** or readers, too. They need to consider what their audience may already know, so they can focus on ideas and content that are new and interesting.

Copyright © 2007 by Holt, Rinehart and Winston. All rights reserved.

Evaluating Ideas and Content

Read the excerpt from a paper below and one reader's comments. The reader has focused on how the writer deals with main idea, details, purpose, and audience. The comments suggest that the writer is on target with main idea, purpose, and audience but not with details.

The main idea—that Dolley Madison is important—is clearly stated.

Although she was not an elected official herself, Dolley Payne Madison, the wife of President James Madison, was an important historical figure. She had a significant influence on the politics of her day and on the history of the United States. Born in Guilford County, North Carolina, in 1768, she grew up in Virginia and married her first husband, a lawyer named John Todd, Jr, in 1790. About a year after Todd's death in 1793, she remarried Congressman James Madison, an outspoken leader, political writer, and future president.

Hmm. These details are about her life, not about her importance.

It was James Madison, along with Alexander Hamilton and John Jay, who authored the famous Federalist papers, a series of letters that spelled out the Federalist philosophy underlying the U.S. Constitution.

These details are about James. Need more details about Dolley.

You can tell that a paper has good ideas when you...

- get the writer's message (the most important idea) right away
- can easily spot and understand the main idea, theme, or story line
- know the writer's purpose for writing
- are interested in what the writer has to say
- pay attention to and can remember the paper's details

When you evaluate another student's paper, you should use the following questions to guide you:

- What is the writer trying to say?
- What is the most important piece of information?
- Do the details support the ideas?
- Are the details interesting and memorable?

Copyright © 2007 by Holt, Rinehart and Winston. All rights reserved.

As you read other papers, use the rubric below to evaluate the writer's ideas and content. (A score of 5 is the highest; a 1 is the lowest score.)

SIX TRAITS RUBRIC: IDEAS AND CONTENT

Score 5	It's Crystal Clear!
A Score 5 paper is clear, focused, and interesting. It presents relevant and concrete details that catch and maintain the reader's interest and support a clear main idea, theme, or story line.	√ The topic is clearly focused—neither too broad nor too narrow—for a paper of its kind. √ The ideas are original, interesting, and creative. √ The writer draws from personal experience or knowledge. √ Key details are insightful and well chosen; they are not obvious, predictable, or clichéd. √ The development of the topic is thorough and logical; the writer anticipates and answers the reader's questions. √ Supporting details are accurate and relevant; every detail contributes to the whole.
Score 3	**Close—It's Getting There**
A Score 3 paper develops the topic in a general or basic way; although clear, the ideas in the paper are routine and lack insight.	√ The topic is underdeveloped, but readers can still understand the writer's purpose and predict how ideas will develop. √ Supporting details are present but can be vague and do not help illustrate the main idea or theme; the writer refers to his or her own experience or knowledge but often fails to push beyond the obvious to more specific ideas. √ Ideas are understandable but not detailed, elaborated upon, or personalized; the writer's ideas do not reveal deep comprehension of the topic or of the writing task. √ The writer does not stray from the topic, but the ideas remain general, forcing readers to rely on what they already know to make sense of the paper; more information is needed to create a complete picture.
Score 1	**Hmm. What Is the Writer Trying to Say?**
A Score 1 paper fails to exhibit any clear purpose or main idea. The reader must infer a coherent and meaningful message from scattered details and incomplete observations.	√ The writer appears not to have decided on a topic or main idea; the paper reads like rough draft or brainstorming notes; it is full of random thoughts. √ The thesis is a vague statement about the topic or a restatement of a prompt, with little or no support, detail, or insight. √ Information is limited and spotty; readers must make inferences to make connections or to identify any organizational pattern. √ The text is rambling and repetitive; ideas are underdeveloped; the paper is too short. √ The paper lacks subordination of ideas; every idea and detail seems equally weighted; ideas are not tied to an overarching thesis or theme.

Copyright © 2007 by Holt, Rinehart and Winston. All rights reserved.

ORGANIZATION

Organization is the way in which writers structure their ideas and content. Writers need to organize their ideas. Without organization, the ideas might seem like a random pile of puzzle pieces. Readers should not have to figure out which idea is most important or see how the ideas connect. A organized paper clearly shows readers how one idea joins the next. As a result, readers understand how all the pieces fit together.

Before you can determine if a piece of writing is organized, you should review the organizational patterns writers may use. The most common patterns are listed below. A writer using

- **chronological order** presents ideas, actions, or events in the order that they take place;
- **spatial order** presents details and information according to location; for example, he or she describes something from near to far, top to bottom, inside to outside, or the reverse;
- **order of importance** arranges ideas from the least to most important, or the reverse;
- **logical order** groups related ideas together.

Usually a writer chooses one main organizational pattern for a paper, but he or she may use more than one. The pattern a writer chooses often depends on the purpose for writing.

For this purpose,	writers may use these organizational patterns:
Expository (to explain)	• *chronological order* to explain the steps in a process or retell historical events • *spatial order* to help readers picture the subject • *order of importance* to explain causes and effects • *logical order* to present groups of related facts or evidence
Persuasive (to convince)	• *order of importance* to present the most persuasive ideas first or last • *logical order* to group related ideas and supporting evidence together
Narrative (to tell a story)	• *chronological order* to tell events in the order that they happen • *spatial order* to help readers imagine an object or setting

Copyright © 2007 by Holt, Rinehart and Winston. All rights reserved.

Evaluating Organization

Read the excerpt from a paper below and one reader's comments about its organizational structure. The reader has focused on how the ideas fit together. The reader's comments suggest that the writer needs to organize the ideas more logically.

> Some people believe that machines may one day be as smart as humans. They point to computers as examples of artificial intelligence. Indeed, computers can do things that humans can do. Others, however, maintain that we will never have true artificial intelligence. But in fact, computers can do many things we can't, such as beat a Russian chess master at his own game, as the IBM computer Deep Blue did in 1997. On the other hand, computers don't really think. They may spell-check a paper quickly, but they can't understand context. As a result, they can't proofread a paper as thoughtfully as an editor. Most computers today would not pass the Turing Test, a series of questions answered by both a computer and a live person. If both answer the question the same way, the computer passes as intelligent.

This paragraph has too many different ideas. I can't follow.

Oh, I get it. The writer is comparing ideas about computers. Not clear though.

This last sentence does not fit here. Logically, it should be in a separate paragraph.

You can tell that a paper has a clear organizational structure when you . . .

- can see connections among the writer's ideas
- can concentrate on the ideas because the connections are clear
- feel that the writer is in control of the way ideas are presented
- feel that the writing has exactly the right pace
- can go back and find information easily because it is logically presented

When you evaluate other papers, you should use the following questions to guide you:

- How are the ideas in the paper organized?
- Does the writer's choice of organizational pattern suit the material?
- Can you see the connections among ideas or do you feel confused?
- Would a change in the way ideas are presented make the paper better?

Copyright © 2007 by Holt, Rinehart and Winston. All rights reserved.

As you read other papers, use the rubric below to evaluate the writer's organization. (A score of 5 is the highest; a 1 is the lowest score.)

SIX TRAITS RUBRIC: ORGANIZATION

Score 5	Yes! I Can See Where This Is Going!
A Score 5 paper uses organizational patterns to clearly communicate a central idea or story line. The order of information draws the reader effortlessly through the text.	√ The paper employs a logical and effective sequence of ideas. √ The paper contains both an attention-grabbing introduction and a satisfying conclusion. √ The pacing is carefully controlled; the writer slows down to provide explanation or elaboration when appropriate, and increases the pace when necessary. √ Transitions make clear connections and cue the reader to specific relationships between ideas. √ The organizational structure is appropriate to the writer's purpose and audience. √ If present, the title sums up the central idea of the paper in a fresh and thoughtful way.
Score 3	**Close—Wait, I Think I Get It**
A Score 3 paper is reasonably strong; it enables readers to move forward without too much confusion.	√ The paper has an introduction and a conclusion. However, the introduction may not be engaging, and the conclusion may not knit together all the paper's ideas. √ The sequence is logical but predictable and therefore not very compelling. √ The sequence may not consistently support the paper's ideas; readers may reorder sections mentally or provide transitions as they read. √ Pacing is reasonably well done, although the writer may move ahead too quickly or linger over unimportant ideas. √ Transitions between ideas may be unclear. √ If present, the title may be dull or lacking insight.
Score 1	**Hmm. I'm a Little Lost**
A Score 1 paper fails to exhibit a sense of purpose or writing strategy; ideas, details, or events seem to be cobbled together without any internal structure or flow.	√ The sequence is broken; one idea or event does not logically follow another; lack of organizational structure, such as clear paragraph breaks, makes it difficult for readers to understand the progression of ideas or events. √ The paper lacks both a clear introduction to guide readers and a conclusion that sums up ideas at the end. √ Pacing is halting or inconsistent; the writer appears not to know when to slow down or speed up the pace. √ Transitions between ideas are confusing or absent. √ If present, the title does not accurately reflect the content of the paper.

Copyright © 2007 by Holt, Rinehart and Winston. All rights reserved.

💬 VOICE

Voice is the way a piece of writing "sounds" to the reader. A writer uses his or her own style to "talk" to readers, and the voice reveals his or her feelings about both the topic and the audience. Voice allows the writer to connect as a person with the reader. Everyone has a natural voice, but good writers are able to tailor their voices to suit their purpose for writing, their topic, and their readers. Here are a couple of examples:

- A writer who is preparing a report (purpose) for the city council (audience) about the effects of building a new shopping center near a local creek (topic) uses a voice that sounds serious, concerned, and informed. He writes in the impersonal third person ("he, she, it") and uses standard English as well specific technological terms.

- A writer who is telling a story (purpose) about visiting her grandfather as a child (topic) for a group of fifth graders (audience) uses a voice that sounds personal, playful, and nostalgic. She writes in the first person ("I") and uses language that is informal. She may try to recreate the voice of the child she once was.

Before you determine if a piece of writing has an appropriate voice, let's review how writers find their voices. Good writers want their voices to appeal to their readers and fit the material. The diagram below shows how writers mix and match their purpose, audience, and voice.

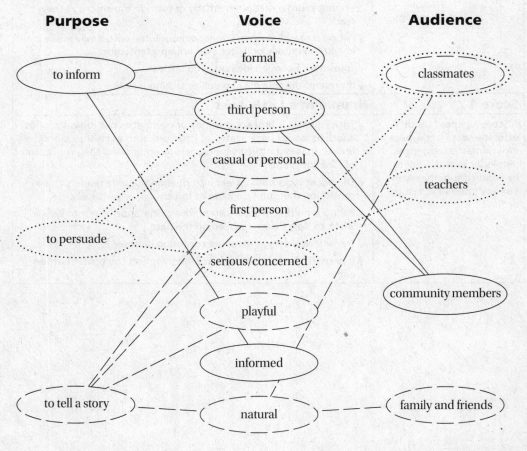

Copyright © 2007 by Holt, Rinehart and Winston. All rights reserved.

Evaluating Voice

Read the first excerpt from a persuasive paper below and one reader's comments about it. The reader has focused on the writer's voice. The first comment suggests that the writer needs to fix his or her voice. Then read the revised version and think about how the new voice has improved the writing.

> The language is informal but the topic is serious. The audience may be, too. The voice is too casual.

Parks should be safe. People enjoying the parks should not have to be stressin' about loose dogs that may mosey up to them. Owners of unleashed dogs are usually somewhere else in the park yakking with their friends instead of paying attention. They are too far away to deal with their lousy dogs. This happens every day at the park next to my house. It probably happens in other parks too, and it's a drag because it messes up the park for everybody.

Parks should be safe. People enjoying the parks should not have to worry about loose dogs that may approach them. Owners of unleashed dogs are usually somewhere else in the park and are unable to effectively control their dogs if they misbehave. This happens every day at the park next to my house, and it is a shame because it ruins the park for everybody.

> Formal language suits the serious topic better. Use of first person is okay; it informs and sounds formal, polite.

You can tell that a paper has a clear and appropriate voice when you...

- feel that the voice "sounds" right
- are aware of and feel connected to the person behind the text
- understand the writer's connection to the topic
- are not distracted by inappropriate language or feelings

When you evaluate another student's paper, you should use the following questions to guide you:

- Does the writer's voice sound right?
- Does the writer's voice suit his or her purpose and audience?
- Is the writer using his or her voice to connect with me?
- Does the writer seem interested in the topic and in me?

Copyright © 2007 by Holt, Rinehart and Winston. All rights reserved.

As you read other papers, use the rubric below to evaluate the writer's voice. (A score of 5 is the highest; a 1 is the lowest score.)

SIX TRAITS RUBRIC:  VOICE

Score 5	**Yes! I Can Really Hear You**
The writing in a Score 5 paper is engaging and conveys the writer's awareness of audience and purpose.	√ The tone of the writing is appropriate for the purpose and audience of the paper. √ The reader is aware of and feels connected to a real person behind the text; if appropriate, the writer takes risks in revealing a personal dimension throughout the piece. √ If the paper is expository or persuasive, the writer shows a strong connection to the topic and explains why readers should care about the issue. √ If the paper is narrative, the point of view is sincere, interesting, and compelling.
Score 3	**Close. Try Again With Feeling**
The writing in a Score 3 paper is reasonably genuine but does not reveal any excitement or connection with the issue; the resulting paper is pleasant but not truly engaging.	√ The writer offers generalities instead of personal insights; as a result, the writing feels impersonal. √ The writer uses neutral language and a flat tone. √ The writer communicates in an earnest and pleasing manner, yet takes no risks; the reader does not feel inspired or engaged. √ Expository or persuasive writing does not reveal the writer's engagement with the topic; there is no attempt to build credibility with the audience. √ Narrative writing fails to reveal a fresh or individual perspective.
Score 1	**Hmm. I Can Barely Hear You**
The writing in a Score 1 paper is mechanical or wooden. The writer appears indifferent to the topic and the audience.	√ The writer shows no concern with the audience; the voice may be inappropriate for the intended reader. √ The development of the topic is so limited that no identifiable point of view is present, or the writing is so short that it offers little but a general introduction of the topic. √ The writer seems to speak in a monotone, using a voice that suppresses all excitement about the message or topic. √ Although the writing may communicate on a functional level, it is ordinary and takes no risks. √ Expository or persuasive writing may lack accurate information or use overly technical language. Narrative writing may lack a point of view and fail to inspire interest.

Copyright © 2007 by Holt, Rinehart and Winston. All rights reserved.

WORD CHOICE

Word choice involves how a writer expresses his or her voice. Words are the building blocks of any piece of writing. The words a writer chooses help create a clear voice and engage the reader. Choosing a precise word is like landing an arrow right in the center of the target.

Word choice makes expository writing more precise, persuasive writing more convincing, and narrative writing more interesting. It helps readers to imagine a scene in a story or to understand the subtle points in a persuasive argument. Without thoughtful word choice, writing is imprecise and dull. Readers become bored and give up.

Before you can determine if a piece of writing contains effective word choices, you may want to review the following terms: **connotation and denotation, idiom, jargon, loaded language,** and **tired or clichéd language.**

- **Connotation and denotation:** The denotation of a word is its definition. The connotation is the feeling associated with the word. Writers should consider the connotations of their word choices.

  Example: Mild *has the denotation of "gentle, not sharp or severe." The feeling associated with it is weakness. Its connotation can be negative or positive. For example, mild weather feels great after a cold winter, but a mild expression conveys a lack of interest.*

- An **idiom** is a phrase that means something different from the words' literal meanings. Idioms are informal. They are great for personal writing or in dialogues in fictional narratives, but they should be avoided in formal writing.

  Examples: *Maria put up with the children. I just don't get it. Never give up.*

- **Jargon** is technical or specialized language that is used by a group of people who share the same profession, occupation, field of study, or hobby. A common word might be jargon. Its meaning may change in different contexts. Jargon works only if the writer knows that the audience will get its meaning. Used properly, jargon conveys the writer's knowledge of a subject.

  Examples: *Stock prices went down. The soup requires chicken stock. The store needs fresh stock.*

- **Loaded language** deliberately provokes a strong reaction from people and reveals a writer's bias. Loaded language works in persuasive writing, but it must be used carefully so as not to offend readers. In narratives, it can be used to show what a character is like.

  Example: *Only people of privilege ride in first class on airplanes. The rest of us are corralled in coach like cattle.*

- **Tired or clichéd words** are phrases and words that have lost their freshness. Writers should avoid clichés and tired words at every opportunity!

  Examples: *The baby's face was as red as a beet. Ah, home sweet home. That was great! You look nice.*

Copyright © 2007 by Holt, Rinehart and Winston. All rights reserved.

Evaluating Word Choice

Read the excerpt from the paper below and one reader's comments. The reader has focused on the writer's choice of words. The comments point out where word choice is effective—and where it is not.

A uniquely American creation in literature is the hard-boiled detective story. Whether in the form of a novel, a short story, a movie, or a television show, the key element in a hard-boiled detective mystery is the characterization. All of the characters in a hard-boiled detective story should be more or less realistic. The forerunners of hard-boiled detective stories were the English drawing-room mysteries. Typically, in these stories, a refined sleuth would brilliantly solve a mysterious murder in a manor house without even breaking a sweat. Such stories are as soothing as a cup of herbal tea and just as stimulating, whereas hard-boiled mysteries are like a punch in the arm.

Hardboiled is jargon. Mystery readers know what it means—dark, realistic mysteries.

"Breaking a sweat" is a cliché. The writer should try "breaking a fingernail."

Refined has negative connotations. It suggests lameness, which conveys the writer's attitude. He doesn't like refined detectives.

Loaded language—you can tell that the writer is biased in favor of the hard-boiled mysteries

You can tell that a paper has made solid word choices when you...

- feel that each word is specific and appropriate
- can say that the language feels natural, not overdone
- do not notice any clichés, jargon, or inappropriate language
- feel engaged by the writing
- are not distracted by words that are confusing or used incorrectly

When you evaluate another student's paper, use the following questions to guide you:

- Why did the writer choose a certain word?
- Would another word have worked better in that sentence?
- Does the language sound natural or appropriate?
- What feelings or ideas does the writer's choice of words suggest?

Copyright © 2007 by Holt, Rinehart and Winston. All rights reserved.

As you read other papers, use the rubric below to evaluate the writer's word choice. (A score of 5 is the highest; a 1 is the lowest score.)

SIX TRAITS RUBRIC: WORD CHOICE

Score 5	Yes! Your Words Come Through Loud and Clear
In a Score 5 paper, words are precise, engaging, and unaffected. They convey the writer's message in an interesting and effective way.	√ All words are specific and appropriate. In all instances, the writer has taken care to choose the right words or phrases. √ The paper's language is natural, not overdone; it never shows a lack of control. Clichés and jargon are rarely used. √ The paper contains energetic verbs; precise nouns and modifiers provide clarity. √ The writer uses vivid words and phrases, including sensory details; such language creates distinct images in the reader's mind.
Score 3	**Close—With a Little Polish Your Words Will Shine**
Despite its lack of flair, the writing in a Score 3 paper gets the message across because it is functional and clear.	√ Words are correct and generally adequate but lack originality or precision. √ Familiar words and phrases do not grab the reader's interest or imagination. Occasional use of lively verbs and phrases perks things up, but the language does not consistently sparkle. √ Attempts at engaging or academic language may seem overly showy or pretentious. √ The writing contains passive verbs and basic nouns and adjectives, and it lacks precise adverbs.
Score 1	**Hmm. I Don't Understand What You Mean**
The limited vocabulary in a Score 1 paper prevents readers from understanding the writer's message. The writer's struggle for words keeps readers from making connections.	√ Vague language communicates an imprecise or incomplete message or understanding of the topic. The reader feels confused and unsure of the writer's purpose. √ Words are used incorrectly. In addition, frequent misuse of parts of speech limits readers' comprehension. √ Excessive repetition or redundancy distracts readers from the message. √ The writing overuses jargon or clichés.

Copyright © 2007 by Holt, Rinehart and Winston. All rights reserved.

SENTENCE FLUENCY

Sentence fluency is how the sentences in a piece of writing flow together. In fact, the word "fluency" comes from the Latin word *fluere*, which means "to flow." Think of a tapestry. A tapestry maker weaves thousands of threads together to create a beautiful pattern or picture. Writing is like a tapestry, with sentences instead of threads. A good writer weaves the sentences together to show the flow of ideas in an interesting way. Unlike tapestry makers, however, writers have to construct their flowing "threads." They must build sentences that are both grammatically correct and interesting. Interesting sentences add rhythm and style to writing. To achieve this rhythm and style, good writers use a mixture of short and long sentences, as well as sentences that start with phrases or clauses, to create a rhythm and style that engages readers.

Before you can determine if a piece of writing has sentence fluency, you should review the following problems that can interfere with it: **sentence fragments, run-on sentences, stringy sentences, choppy sentences,** and **wordy sentences.**

- A **sentence fragment** is a group of words that has been capitalized and punctuated as if it were a complete sentence, but it may a subject, a verb, or both. **Examples:** *Finished his homework.* (lacks a noun) *Then he dinner.* (lacks a verb) *Before Dad came home.* (lacks noun and verb) Sentence fragments interrupt sentence fluency and are grammatically incorrect. Readers must puzzle out the writer's meaning—*Toby finished his homework. Then he made dinner before Dad came home.*

- **Run-on sentences** run two or more sentences together as if they were one. **Example:** *People who want to adopt a puppy should visit a local animal shelter shelters always have puppies that need good homes.* (The sentence has two ideas—people should visit shelters, and shelters have puppies.) Run-ons are grammatically incorrect and confuse readers. They can't tell where one idea ends and another begins.

- **Stringy sentences** have too many ideas strung together with conjunctions and transition words. **Example:** *My grandmother dreamed of becoming a teacher, but she was poor, but then she won a scholarship, so she attended a college, and she found a job right away.* Stringy sentences are confusing because the reader can't tell which idea is most important.

- **Choppy sentences** are very short. **Examples:** *I love cheese. I like pickles. I eat pickle and cheese sandwiches.* A series of short, choppy sentences disrupts the flow of ideas and does not tell which idea is most important.

- **Wordy sentences** use more words than are necessary to express an idea. **Examples:** *I was late for school because <u>of the fact that</u> I missed the bus. When I got to <u>the very end of</u> the book, I wrote my report.* The extra words get in the readers' way. Readers may edit them out—"I was late for school because I missed the bus." "When I finished the book, I wrote my report."

Copyright © 2007 by Holt, Rinehart and Winston. All rights reserved.

Evaluating Sentence Fluency

Read the excerpt from the paper below and one reader's comments about it. The reader has focused on the paper's sentence fluency. The comments point out where sentences flow well and where they do not.

Good fluency. A mix of short and long sentences. The sentences are grammatically correct.

Vegetarians need to eat a variety of foods. Fruits, fresh vegetables, whole grain breads, cereal, and legumes (such as dried beans and peas) are the foods basic to good health. Experts once worried that vegetarians didn't get enough protein most should get all the protein they need from a varied diet. Most people don't have balanced diets. Even meat eaters. People should take vitamins. They should eat more carefully. When vegetarians eat a balance of foods, they are as healthy as any meat-eater.

Run-on sentence. Two independent clauses appear in one sentence without a conjunction.

Whoa! Choppy sentences! "Even meat eaters" is a fragment. Which idea is important?

This is the only sentence that starts with a clause. It's interesting and makes a clear point.

You can tell that a paper has sentence fluency when you...

- understand the writer's meaning and see connections between ideas
- understand which idea is most important
- feel engaged by the writing
- appreciate the rhythm and style of the sentences
- notice the variety of sentence beginnings and lengths

When you evaluate another student's paper, use the following questions to guide you:

- Does the writing feel natural as it flows from one idea to the next?
- Are the sentences interesting and grammatically correct?
- Do the sentences express ideas and make clear connections?
- Do the sentences have rhythm and style?

Copyright © 2007 by Holt, Rinehart and Winston. All rights reserved.

As you read other papers, use the rubric below to evaluate the writer's sentence fluency. (A score of 5 is the highest; a 1 is the lowest score.)

SIX TRAITS RUBRIC:  SENTENCE FLUENCY

Score 5	Yes! The Sentences Really Flow
Sentences in a Score 5 paper are thoughtfully constructed, and sentence structure is varied throughout. When read aloud, the writing is fluent and rhythmic.	√ The writer constructs sentences so that meaning is clear to the reader. √ Sentences vary in length and in structure. √ Varied sentence beginnings add interest and clarity. √ The writing has a steady rhythm; the reader is able to read the text effortlessly without confusion or stumbling. √ Dialogue, if used, is natural. Any fragments are used purposefully and contribute to the paper's style. √ Thoughtful connectives and transitions between sentences reveal how the papers' ideas work together.
Score 3	Close—But I Feel As Though I'm Drifting Off Course
The text of a Score 3 paper maintains a steady rhythm but the reader may find it flat or mechanical rather than fluent or musical.	√ Sentences are usually grammatical and unified, but they are routine rather than artful. The writer has not paid a great deal of attention to how the sentences sound. √ There is some variation in sentence length and structure as well as in sentence beginnings. Not all sentences are constructed exactly the same way. √ The reader may have to search for transitional words and phrases that show how sentences relate to one another. Sometimes, such context clues are entirely absent when they should be present. √ Although sections of the paper invite expressive oral reading, the reader may also encounter many stilted or awkward sections.
Score 1	Hmm. I'm a Little Lost
The reader of a Score 1 paper will encounter challenges in reading the choppy or confusing text; meaning may be significantly obscured by the errors in sentence construction.	√ The sentences do not "hang together." They are run-on, incomplete, monotonous, or awkward. √ Phrasing often sounds too singsong, not natural. The paper does not allow for expressive oral reading. √ Nearly all the sentences begin the same way, and they may all follow the same pattern (e.g. subject-verb-object). The end result may be a monotonous repetition of sounds. √ Endless connectives or a complete lack of connectives creates a confused muddle of language.

Copyright © 2007 by Holt, Rinehart and Winston. All rights reserved.

CONVENTIONS

Conventions are the agreed rules of paragraphing, usage, grammar, spelling, and punctuation that good writers follow. Conventions help writers make their meanings clear. Think how difficult it would be to read another person's paper if people were allowed to make up their own rules of spelling, punctuation, and grammar.

A writer should always edit and proofread a paper for mistakes in conventions because even small mistakes can distract or confuse a reader. You want your readers to focus on your words and ideas. Still, conventional errors can slip by. Here is a checklist that can help you catch them.

Paragraphing
___ Is each paragraph indented?
___ Does each paragraph focus on just one main idea?
___ Does the paragraph break in a logical place? (If not, where should it break?)

Grammar and Usage
___ Does every sentence have both a subject and a verb?
___ Do the subject(s) and verb(s) in each sentence agree?
___ Are the correct forms of irregular verbs and personal pronouns used?
___ Are there any double-negatives? (If so, how should they be corrected?)

Punctuation and Capitalization
___ Does each sentence end with correct punctuation?
___ Are commas and semicolons used correctly?
___ Are proper nouns capitalized?
___ Does each sentence and direct quotation begin with a capital letter?
___ Are apostrophes used to indicate possession or missing letters?

Spelling
___ Are words that sound alike but are spelled differently spelled correctly?
___ Are commonly misspelled words spelled correctly?
___ Are proper nouns and place names spelled correctly?

Just in case you find conventional errors in the papers you read, use the editing and proofreading marks shown below to make corrections.

Symbols for Editing and Proofreading

Symbol	Example	Meaning of Symbol
≈	at Emerson lake	Capitalize a lowercase letter.
/	a gift for my Aunt	Lowercase a capital letter.
∧	costs *thirty* cents	Insert a missing word, letter, or punctuation mark.
⌐	near *our* their house	Replace something.
℈	What time is is it?	Leave out a word, letter, or punctuation mark.
∿	recieved	Change the order of the letters.
¶	¶ The third effect is...	Begin a new paragraph.
⊙	Please sit down⊙	Add a period.
∧	Yes, I heard you.	Add a comma.

Copyright © 2007 by Holt, Rinehart and Winston. All rights reserved.

Evaluating the Use of Conventions

Read the excerpt from the paper below and one reader's corrections. The reader has focused on the writer's use of conventions.

There
~~Their~~ are several types of prejudice, such as social,

political, and racial prejudices. Everyone ~~are~~ *is* prejudice*d*

against some sort of thing. It might be food, cars, races

of people, etc. I believe to overcome prejudice is to not

show your feelings towards something you are preju-

diced about. If you are prejudiced against someone's

nationality without even personally meeting this person,

~~I think~~ that is wrong ~~or~~ if one person is a c*e*rtain race,

and they commit a crime, don't ~~never~~ think everyone

of that race is exactly like that. Everyone has *his or her* ~~their~~ own

personality. I believe that you should welcome

everyone instead of saying you don't like someone

because of nationality or race.

You can tell that a paper has correct conventions when you...
- do not see any conventional errors
- feel that the writer's meaning is clear and not affected by small errors
- feel that the writer has excellent control of conventions

When you evaluate another student's paper, use the following questions to guide you:
- Do I notice any conventional errors?
- Do the conventional errors interfere with my understanding?
- Does the writer need to brush up on the rules of grammar, usage, or punctuation?
- Does the writer need to remember to use a dictionary or a spell-checker?

Copyright © 2007 by Holt, Rinehart and Winston. All rights reserved.

As you read other papers, use the rubric below to evaluate the writer's conventions. (A score of 5 is the highest; a 1 is the lowest score.)

SIX TRAITS RUBRIC: CONVENTIONS

Score 5	It's Nearly Perfect!
Standard writing conventions in a Score 5 paper are used correctly and in a way that aids the reader's understanding. Any errors tend to be minor; the piece is nearly ready for publication.	√ Paragraphing is regular and enhances the organization of the paper. √ Grammar and usage are correct and add clarity to the text as a whole. Sometimes the writer may manipulate conventions in a controlled way—especially grammar and spelling—for stylistic effect. √ Punctuation is accurate; it enables the reader to move though the text with understanding and ease. √ The writer's understanding of capitalization rules is evident throughout the paper. √ Most words, even difficult ones, are spelled correctly. √ The writing is long and complex enough to show the writer using a wide range of convention skills successfully.
Score 3	**Close—I Found a Few Errors**
The writer of a Score 3 paper exhibits an awareness of a limited set of standard writing conventions and uses them to enhance the papers' readability. Some errors distract and confuse readers. Moderate editing is required before publication.	√ Paragraphs are used but may begin in the wrong places, or sections that should be separate paragraphs are run together. √ Conventions may not always be correct; however, problems with grammar and usage are usually not serious enough to distort meaning. √ End marks are usually correct, but other punctuation marks, such as commas, apostrophes, semi-colons, and parentheses, may be missing or wrong. √ Common words are usually spelled correctly. √ Most words are capitalized correctly, but the writer's command of capitalization skills is inconsistent.
Score 1	**Hmm. I'm Distracted By Too Many Errors**
In a Score 1 paper there are errors in spelling, punctuation, grammar and usage, and paragraphing that seriously impede the reader's comprehension. Extensive editing is required for publication.	√ Paragraphing is missing, uneven, or too frequent. Most of the paragraphs do not reinforce or support the organizational structure of the paper. √ Errors in grammar and usage are very common and distracting; such errors also affect the paper's meaning. √ Punctuation, including terminal punctuation, is often missing or incorrect. √ Even common words are frequently misspelled. √ Capitalization is haphazard or reveals the writer's understanding of only the simplest rules. √ The paper must be read once just to decode the language and then again to capture the paper's meaning.

Copyright © 2007 by Holt, Rinehart and Winston. All rights reserved.

As you read other papers, use this at-a-glance rubric to evaluate the writer's use of all of the six traits. (A score of 5 is the highest; a 1 is the lowest score.)

SIX TRAITS: **AT-A-GLANCE**

Ideas and Content	Organization	Voice
5 The paper is clear and focused, with ideas that engage the reader.	**5** The organizational structure suits the content and connects ideas.	**5** The writer's personality is clear and engaging.
√ The topic is clearly focused for a paper of its kind. √ The ideas are original, interesting, and creative. √ The writer draws from personal experience. √ Key details are insightful and well chosen. √ The development of the topic is thorough and logical. √ Supporting details are accurate and relevant.	√ The paper employs a logical and effective sequence of ideas. √ The paper contains both an introduction and a conclusion. √ The pacing is carefully controlled. √ Transitions make clear connections and cue the reader to relationships between ideas. √ The organizational structure is appropriate to the writer's purpose and audience.	√ The tone of the writing is appropriate for the purpose and audience of the paper. √ The reader is aware of and feels connected to a real person behind the text. √ If the paper is expository or persuasive, the writer shows a strong connection to the topic and tells why readers should care. √ If the paper is narrative, the point of view is sincere, interesting, and compelling.
3 The ideas are vague and not fully thought out.	**3** The organization is clear but readers may get confused.	**3** The writer is sincere but not completely engaged.
√ The topic is underdeveloped but readers can still understand the writer's purpose. √ Supporting details are present but can be vague and do not help illustrate the main idea or theme. √ Ideas are understandable but not detailed, elaborated upon, or personalized. √ The ideas remain general; more information is needed to create a complete picture.	√ The paper has an introduction and conclusion. √ The sequence is logical but predictable and therefore not very compelling. √ The sequence may not consistently support the paper's ideas. √ Pacing is reasonably well done. √ Transitions between ideas may be unclear.	√ The writer offers generalities that feel impersonal. √ The writer uses neutral language and a slightly flattened tone. √ The writer communicates in an earnest and pleasing manner, yet takes no risks. √ Expository or persuasive writing does not reveal a engagement with the topic. √ Narrative writing fails to reveal a fresh or individual perspective.
1 The paper lacks clear ideas and purpose.	**1** The paper fails to make connections and show the big picture.	**1** The writer seems uninvolved in the topic and the reader.
√ The paper reads like rough draft or brainstorming notes. √ The thesis is a vague statement about the topic or a restatement of a prompt, with little or no support, detail. √ Information is limited and spotty; readers must make inferences.	√ One idea or event does not logically follow another; lack of organizational structure makes it difficult for readers to understand the progression of ideas or events. √ The paper lacks both a clear introduction and a conclusion. √ Pacing is halting or inconsistent. √ Transitions between ideas are confusing or absent.	√ The writer shows no concern with the audience. √ The writing lacks a point of view. √ The writer seems to speak in a monotone. √ The writing is ordinary and takes no risks. √ Expository or persuasive writing may lack accurate information. Narrative writing may lack a point of view and fail to interest.

Copyright © 2007 by Holt, Rinehart and Winston. All rights reserved.

EVALUATING AN EXPOSITORY ESSAY USING
THE SIX WRITING TRAITS

Directions A student is to respond to the expository prompt below. In it, the
student is asked to write a completed evaluation on the next page. Then, answer
the questions...

Word Choice	Sentence Fluency	Conventions
5 The words bring the paper to life and engage the reader. √ All words are specific and appropriate. The writer chooses the right words or phrases. √ The paper's language is natural, and controlled. Clichés and jargon appear rarely. √ The paper contains energetic verbs; precise nouns and modifiers provide clarity. √ The writer uses vivid words and phrases, including sensory details.	**5 The sentences are varied and interesting.** √ The writer constructs sentences so that meaning is clear. √ Sentences vary in length and in structure. √ Varied sentence beginnings add interest and clarity. √ The reader is able to read the text effortlessly without confusion. √ Dialogue, if used, is natural. Fragments are used purposefully. √ Thoughtful connectives and transitions between sentences bring the ideas together.	**5 The writing is clear and uses correct spelling, punctuation, and grammar.** √ Paragraphing is regular and enhances the organization of the paper. √ Grammar and usage are correct and add clarity to the text. √ Punctuation is accurate. √ The writer understands the rules of capitalization rules. √ Most words, even difficult ones, are spelled correctly. √ The writing shows a wide range of convention skills successfully.
3 The language is clear but uninspired. √ Words are correct and adequate but lack originality or precision. √ Familiar words and phrases do not grab the reader's interest or imagination. The language does not consistently sparkle. √ Attempts at engaging language may seem showy. √ The writing contains passive verbs and basic nouns and adjectives, and it lacks precise adverbs.	**3 The sentences make sense but the connections are not clear.** √ Sentences are usually grammatical, but they are routine rather than artful. √ There is some variation in sentence length and structure as well as in sentence beginnings. √ The reader may have to search for transitional words and phrases that show how sentences relate to one another. √ The reader may also encounter many stilted or awkward sections.	**3 Basic punctuation, grammar, and spelling are employed, but there are some mistakes.** √ Paragraphs are used but may begin in the wrong places. √ Conventions may not always be correct; however, problems are not serious enough to distort meaning. √ End marks are usually correct, but other punctuation marks, such as commas, apostrophes, semi-colons, and parentheses, may be missing or wrong. √ Common words are usually spelled correctly. √ Most words are capitalized correctly, but capitalization skills is inconsistent.
1 The language is used incorrectly or ineffectively. √ Vague language communicates an incomplete message or understanding of the topic. The reader feels confused and unsure of the writer's purpose. √ Words are used incorrectly. √ Excessive repetition distracts readers from the message. √ The writing overuses jargon or clichés.	**1 The sentences are awkward and do not connect ideas.** √ The sentences do not "hang together;" they are run-on, incomplete, or awkward. √ Phrasing often sounds too singsong, not natural. √ Nearly all the sentences begin the same way, and they may all follow the same pattern (e.g. subject-verb-object). √ Endless connectives or a lack of connectives creates a confused muddle of language.	**1 The paper contains many errors that interfere with the meaning.** √ Paragraphing is missing, uneven, or too frequent. √ Errors in grammar and usage are common and distracting, and affect the paper's meaning. √ Punctuation, including end marks, is often missing or incorrect. √ Even common words are frequently misspelled. √ Capitalization reveals the writer's understanding of only the simplest rules. √ The paper must be read once just to decode the language and then again to capture the paper's meaning.

Copyright © 2007 by Holt, Rinehart and Winston. All rights reserved.

EVALUATING AN EXPOSITORY ESSAY USING THE SIX WRITING TRAITS

Directions: A student responded to the expository prompt below. Read the student's essay and the completed evaluation on the next page. Then, answer the questions that follow.

> **Expository Prompt:** *"I have a dream that my four little children will one day live in a nation where they will not be judged by the color of their skin but by the content of their character."* Write an essay explaining what you think Dr. Martin Luther King, Jr. means in this quotation. You may use examples from real life, books, movies, or television shows.

    It does not matter what color people are, how they, dress, what kind of car they drive, or how big the house is in which they live. A person should be judged by his or her responsibility. A white man can have the same morals as a black man. Their principles can be identical. They can both be angels, or just as likely they can be cowardly heathens.

    A person's color does not gaurantee that their personality and demeanor will fit into a certain, forechosen category. Just because a person's skin color is white does not mean that he or she is a good person. Or that a black person is a criminal. Take the case of Ruben "Hurricane" Carter. He was convicted of murder and spent several years in prison based on absolutely no evidence of any kind. The all-white jury convicted him solely on the fact that he was black. He could have been the boxing champion of the world. Instead he was sent to prison where his health deteriorated. Literature provides us with many illustrations of racial stereotyping. For example, Tom Robinson , the main black character in To Kill a Mockingbird, was accused of a very serious crime against a white person. During the trial it became clear that the charges were not at all true. The defense lawyer, Atticus Finch, stated that Tom's only crime was to feel sorry for and to help a white person. In other words, Tom's real offense was the color of his skin.

    A person should be judged based on their responsibility, clearheadedness, and their ability to determine and do the right thing. A man cannot be juadged by the fact that he cannot walk, needs glasses to see, is not six feet tall, or needs a hearing aid. A man can only be judged by close examination of his scruples, morals, principles, and judgement. When a man is judged on unimportant qualities, it should be a crime. We will never forget the attempt by Nazi Germany to weed out people who were considered to be weak or flawed.

Copyright © 2007 by Holt, Rinehart and Winston. All rights reserved.

Although the Nazis seemed superiour, they possessed the true flaws.

Martin Luther King, Jr. fought hard to instill this kind of thinking into his family and into everyone around him. He died fighting for this idea to be heard. He gave his life to try and teach the world about respect, decency, friendship, and most of all love between races. We should all try and learn from his words of wisdom.

Copyright © 2007 by Holt, Rinehart and Winston. All rights reserved.

One Reader's Evaluation

A reader used the six trait rubrics on pp. 20–21 to evaluate the preceding expository essay. Below are her scores and comments.

Expository Essay: Six Trait Scores	
Ideas and Content	5
Organization	4
Voice	5
Word Choice	3
Sentence Fluency	4
Conventions	5

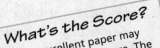

What's the Score?
Even an excellent paper may not get 5's for every score. The point of scoring the traits is not to get an overall score or grade. It is to see which traits are strong for a writer and which need more work.

One Reader's Comments:

Ideas and Content: The paper clearly responds to the prompt and stays focused on the topic of prejudice. The examples from life, history, and literature are accurate, interesting, and compelling. The writer has clear ideas about prejudice.

Organization: Overall, the organization is good. The essay has a clear introduction and conclusion. The writer could use more transitions to help readers follow the flow of examples.

Voice: The writer clearly feels strongly about the topic. I feel that the writer is clearly speaking in his or her own voice and is willing to take risks in expressing ideas.

Word Choice: Although the writer is earnest, his or her choice of words is often too general. Some words like *demeanor* and *scruples* fit nicely, but *forechosen* is a bit of a stretch. The writer uses "big idea" words that could be more specific.

Sentence Fluency: The sentence structure is varied, which creates an interesting rhythm and keeps readers going. Some sentences have awkward or repetitive phrasing: ". . . based on absolutely no evidence of any kind."

Conventions: The writer demonstrates a fair understanding of conventions. Although there are some stray commas and spelling errors, they do not interfere with the writer's meaning.

Sum It Up: Overall I thought the paper was coherent, thoughtful, and engaging. I could tell the writer cared deeply about the message that prejudice is bad.

Copyright © 2007 by Holt, Rinehart and Winston. All rights reserved.

Your Turn

Now answer the questions below. Use the rubrics on pp. 20-21 to figure out how you would score the essay on the previous page. How do your responses compare to the scores shown above?

1. I do/ do not agree with the evaluator's score on the writer's ideas and contents because

_____

_____

2. I do/ do not agree with the evaluator's score on the writer's organization because

_____

_____

3. I do/ do not agree with the evaluator's score on the writer's voice because

_____

_____

4. I do/ do not agree with the evaluator's score on the writer's word choice because

_____

_____

5. I do/ do not agree with the evaluator's score on the writer's sentence fluency because

_____

_____

6. I do/ do not agree with the evaluator's score on the writer's conventions because

_____

_____

7. If you were to give the essay different scores from the ones on p. 24, what would they be? Why do you think different scores should be given?

_____

_____

Copyright © 2007 by Holt, Rinehart and Winston. All rights reserved.

EVALUATING A PERSUASIVE ESSAY USING THE SIX WRITING TRAITS

Directions: A student responded to the persuasive prompt below. Read the student's essay and the completed evaluation on the next page. Then, answer the questions that follow.

> **Persuasive Prompt:** *Imagine that a local builder found an ancient campsite while clearing land to build a badly needed school. Should the builder be allowed to proceed, or should building stop while archaeologists study the site? Local schools are overcrowded, and archaeologists estimate that it could take as long as a year to complete their study. Write an essay for your school newspaper in which you state your position on this issue and support it with convincing reasons and details.*

    If construction of a new school for our city is suspended for a year, as archaeologists want, some classes in our old school will have fifty or more students next year. I know it is important to make discoveries at the ancient campsite, but I think a year is too long to wait to start building a new school. I think we should give the archaeologists a shorter time to dig so we don't spend another whole year crowded into an old building and trailers. I believe that technology can help both projects get done faster and that people on both sides want the best for history and for children.

    Technology can help in two ways. I think the archaeologists should get one of those machines that lets them see objects underground. If they see anything out of the ordinary, they should start digging immediately. If they find nothing in a period of five months, we should start to build the foundation for our new school. During the time when the archaeologists are looking at the site, the new school can be designed, and we can use computer programs to plan and figure out the most efficient way to do the job. That way, as soon as the archaeologists finish, we can be ready to start work right away and finish the school more quickly.

    If I were an archaeologist, of course I would want to dig up whatever treasure is underground. They might learn more about early humans or maybe even find something that can confirm the way dinosaurs died, and then they would want to keep digging. Still, if I were an archaeologist, I would probably want the best for the children. After all, archaeologists spent a lot of time in school. They know it's important. They might even have kids, too. The archaeologists should try to finish their project as soon as they can so that the school will be

Copyright © 2007 by Holt, Rinehart and Winston. All rights reserved.

ready by the next school year. If I were an archaeologist, I would not want my work to force kids to stay crowded in an old school.

On the other hand, if I were an administrator, obviously I would want to build the school. However, I would probably be interested in finding out what was at the site, too. If there were fossils or artifacts to be found, I would have the archaeologists start digging. Their discoveries might give us further things to study in our new school, and our school would be recognized as the place where an important discovery was made. Finding fossils at our new school will give us an advantage, but stopping construction for a whole year would mean the old school will still be crowded and put the students at a disadvantage.

The best solution to this problem is to limit the delay caused by digging at the site. The archaeologists and builders should use technology to speed up the process so that construction of the new school can begin in time for the school to be ready for the next school year. We deserve to go to a new school that is not overcrowded.

Copyright © 2007 by Holt, Rinehart and Winston. All rights reserved.

One Reader's Evaluation

A reader used the rubrics on pp. 20–21 to evaluate the persuasive essay above. Below are her scores and comments.

Persuasive Essay: Six Trait Scores	
Ideas and Content	4
Organization	5
Voice	4
Word Choice	3
Sentence Fluency	5
Conventions	5

What's the Score?
Sometimes a trait in a paper may deserve a score of a 4 or a 2. The rubrics don't show those scores, though. Use your judgment. If you think that a paper's organization is not quite a 5 but definitely better than a 3, you can always give a score of 4.

One Reader's Comments

Ideas and Content: The writer identifies a clear position and considers multiple perspectives, although the ideas sometimes lack specificity.

Organization: Organization fits the writer's purpose, and ideas progress logically.

Voice: The writer demonstrates a keen involvement with the topic, but uses a fair and calm voice as he or she discusses possible concerns from opposing viewpoints.

Word Choice: Word choice is correct and adequate to communicate the writer's ideas.

Sentence Fluency: Sentences vary in length and structure and clearly communicate the writer's message.

Conventions: The writer demonstrates control over the conventions of written language; paragraphing, grammar, punctuation, capitalization, and spelling are generally correct.

Sum It Up: Overall I thought the paper was balanced, thoughtful, and interested in the topic. I could tell the writer cared deeply about both building a new school and making historical discoveries.

Copyright © 2007 by Holt, Rinehart and Winston. All rights reserved.

Your Turn

Now answer the questions below. Use the rubrics on pp. 20–21 to figure out how you would score the preceding persuasive essay (pp. 26–27). How do your responses compare to the scores shown above?

1. I do/ do not agree with the evaluator's score on the writer's ideas and contents because

_____

_____

2. I do/ do not agree with the evaluator's score on the writer's organization because

_____

_____

3. I do/ do not agree with the evaluator's score on the writer's voice because

_____

_____

4. I do/ do not agree with the evaluator's score on the writer's word choice because

_____

_____

5. I do/ do not agree with the evaluator's score on the writer's sentence fluency because

_____

_____

6. I do/ do not agree with the evaluator's score on the writer's conventions because

_____

_____

7. If you were to give the essay different scores from the ones on p. 28, what would they be? Why do you think different scores should be given?

_____

_____

Copyright © 2007 by Holt, Rinehart and Winston. All rights reserved.

EVALUATING A NARRATIVE ESSAY USING THE SIX WRITING TRAITS

Directions: A student responded to the narrative prompt below. Read the student's essay and the completed evaluation on the next page. Then, answer the questions that follow.

> **Narrative Prompt:** *Think of an important event or incident in your life. What lesson did you learn? Write a well-developed personal narrative that describes the experience and reveals why it was important to you.*

Sometimes my imagination takes off too quickly. One day my parents, my sister Elena, and I were driving to Virginia for a long weekend. I was looking at a brochure for the place we were going to stay. "Hey, Mom," I said, "they have hot-air balloon rides." Dad asked whether we would like to try it. Without hesitating, I said, "Sure." Mom offered to call for reservations. "Goody," squealed Elena.

I imagined the balloon ride. What had I been thinking? I had agreed to go up in a little basket attached to a balloon. "There is no way of steering the vehicle," the brochure explained, "so it just goes with the wind." Panic set in. I comforted myself with the thought that Mom probably couldn't get reservations so late.

When we got to the hotel, Mom called about the balloon ride. Elena stood beside her, looking eager. I was thinking, "Please say you don't have room for us." Mom got off the phone and announced cheerfully, "We meet the balloonist at 6:30a.m." Elena was thrilled. I was imagining what my friends would say when they heard how I had drifted away into the pillowy clouds or worse, slammed into a building.

I tossed and turned all night and dreamed of crash landings in the desert. Never mind that there are no deserts in Virginia. Finally, morning came. My last hope was that it would rain, but a peek out the window took away that hope. Soon people would be rescuing me from a tree.

We waited outside. My fears quadrupled when I saw the balloonist drive up. The basket on the back of the truck couldn't possibly hold all of us. We drove to a field as the sun popped over the horizon. The team prepared the balloon. Everyone else in my family was fascinated. I felt sick. Finally, we climbed into the tiny basket with the balloon pilot. Once we were settled, the team let go of the ropes. In no time, we were softly gliding upward over the velvety, rolling hills. "Hey, this is great!" I yelled. I had to laugh when I realized how much time I had wasted worrying. Sometimes I need to listen to my imagination.

Copyright © 2007 by Holt, Rinehart and Winston. All rights reserved.

One Reader's Evaluation

A reader used the rubrics on pp. 20–21 to evaluate the narrative essay above. Below are her scores and comments.

Narrative Essay: Six Trait Scores	
Ideas and Content	5
Organization	5
Voice	5
Word Choice	5
Sentence Fluency	5
Conventions	5

A Closer Look

Think about the writer's purpose when you give scores for organization. For example, the purpose of a narrative is to tell a story. Usually the events should be organized in the order that they occur. If they are out of order or hard to follow, you need to give a lower score for organization.

One Reader's Comments

Ideas and Content: A clear idea—overcoming fear—governs the narrative. The reader receives a clear idea of the character of the narrator and his or her sister. Appropriate details about the parents are required for plot development. The writer obviously learned a lesson and shares it with the readers.

Organization: The organizational structure effectively incorporates internal dialogue and suspense to move the plot along, and the narrative builds to an effective resolution that suggests a lesson about life.

Voice: The writer's voice is clear and engaging and demonstrates a thoughtful approach to the writing task.

Word Choice: Word choice is specific and effective.

Sentence Fluency: The narrative uses a variety of sentence types and structures. The sentences flowed nicely and had a nice pace, speeding up or slowing down the action as appropriate.

Conventions: The writer demonstrates a strong command of the conventions of the English language.

Sum It Up: Overall I thought the paper was insightful, clear, and fun to read. I could tell the writer understood how the experience affected his or her life.

Copyright © 2007 by Holt, Rinehart and Winston. All rights reserved.

Your Turn

Now answer the questions below. Use the rubrics on pp. 20–21 to figure out how you would score the preceding narrative essay (p. 30). How do your responses compare to the scores shown above?

1. I do/ do not agree with the evaluator's score on the writer's ideas and contents because

_____

_____

2. I do/ do not agree with the evaluator's score on the writer's organization because

_____

_____

3. I do/ do not agree with the evaluator's score on the writer's voice because

_____

_____

4. I do/ do not agree with the evaluator's score on the writer's word choice because

_____

_____

5. I do/ do not agree with the evaluator's score on the writer's sentence fluency because.

_____

_____

6. I do/ do not agree with the evaluator's score on the writer's conventions because

_____

_____

7. If you were to give the essay different scores from the ones on p. 31, what would they be? Why do you think different scores should be given?

_____

_____

Copyright © 2007 by Holt, Rinehart and Winston. All rights reserved.

PRACTICE ESSAYS AND STUDENT EVALUATION SHEETS

Expository Essay: Read the prompt and the expository essay below. Then review the Six Trait rubrics on pp. 20–21. Use the blank evaluation form that follows to score the writer's work.

> **Expository Prompt:** *Jeannette Rankin was the first woman ever elected to the United States Congress. She was a dedicated pacifist, a person who opposed war. She is famous for stating, "You can no more win a war than you can win an earthquake." Write an essay in which you explain what you think Rankin meant in this quotation. You may use examples from real life as well as from books, movies, or television shows.*

War and earthquakes are alike in many ways. I think Ms. Rankin is saying that war and earthquakes are alike in that they both produce the same results. Both of them end up with the same kinds of disasters and have a major impact on the world. When a war starts, no one is sure how it will end, but they know that the results are usually bad. Buildings are destroyed and people are killed. An earthquake is just like that because when it starts you have no idea when it will end, or what problems it will produce. But when it is over, it has caused a lot of damage. You really cannot win either way you look at it. Even if you win a war, many things are lost in the process.

War is like an earthquake in another way. Both of them are unpredictable. You never know when they are coming. Scientists study earthquakes and what causes them. But they still can't predict them very well. Earthquakes are happening every day in the world. Some of them you don't feel or hear about, but the ones you do hear about have the greatest impact on our lives. In California, the worst earthquakes happen and their effects are all over the news—how many were killed or injured, what houses or buildings were lost, and which roads were destroyed.

America has won a lot of wars in the past, but we lost so much in the process. Think of all the names carved into the walls of the Vietnam Memorial. Think of all the prisoners of war and what they went through. What about their families? You should not start something unless you have a positive feeling about it. Right now everybody is wondering if the United States will ever get out of Iraq. Nobody knows how many people will be killed or what we will lose forever. Earthquakes are similar. There is no winning either of the two.

Copyright © 2007 by Holt, Rinehart and Winston. All rights reserved.

Directions: In the table below, write the scores you give the expository essay for its execution of six writing traits. (The highest score is 5; the lowest is 1.)

Expository Essay: My Scores	
Ideas and Content	
Organization	
Voice	
Word Choice	
Sentence Fluency	
Conventions	

Directions: Below write some comments that explain the scores you wrote above. Use specific examples from the text to support your evaluations.

My Comments

Ideas and Content: _____

_____

_____

Organization: _____

_____

_____

Voice: _____

_____

_____

Word Choice: _____

_____

_____

Sentence Fluency: _____

_____

_____

Conventions: _____

_____

_____

Sum It Up: _____

_____

_____

Copyright © 2007 by Holt, Rinehart and Winston. All rights reserved.

Persuasive Essay: Read the prompt and the persuasive essay below. Then review the Six Trait rubrics on pp. 20–21. Use the blank evaluation form that follows to score the writer's work.

Persuasive Prompt: *Are school uniforms a restriction on individual freedom? Do uniforms help maintain discipline and reduce the pressure to wear the "right" clothes? Write a well-organized paper in which you state and give reasons for your opinion on this issue.*

Are school uniforms a restriction on individual freedom? Do uniforms help to maintain discipline and reduce the pressure to wear the "right" clothes?

Some say yes, some say no. Individual freedom is defined as the freedom that an individual has. Also discipline is defined as the rules a person must obey or be punished. "Right" clothes is defined as what everybody says is cool. You have to wear clothes to school to be cool. Not everybody likes uniforms. Certainly not me.

If a person is acting up in the hall and showing off, the teacher could tell that person to put on a uniform, and he would be discipled. But what would he do with the clothes he wore to school? His freedoms would be taken away.

At our school an assist. principle tells the girls all the time there have too short skirts but they just laugh at him. If they complain, he tells the parents.

One friend tole me she has school uniforms at her school. She think they are terrible. That school won't let them do anything. Not even to their hair. She says when school is out, she is going to throw uniform in the trash. She never will wear black and blue again. At her school the uniforms are not even the school colors, which are gold and purple. Their team is called the Bruins and the football team has a cool uniform. Not like my friend who has a terrible uniform because they make her wear it.

We need our freedom because we will learn to drive soon and be in high school. Even with uniforms we need freedom. We need to take care of uniforms ourselves. But I am not sure how. What do you think—uniforms or no uniforms?

In conclusion, it may be a restriction of individual rights and freedoms. Or a disciple maintainer, or to avoid the peer pressure. What is right for you, you do.

Copyright © 2007 by Holt, Rinehart and Winston. All rights reserved.

Directions: In the table below, write the scores you give the persuasive essay for its execution of six writing traits. (The highest score is 5; the lowest is 1.)

Persuasive Essay: My Scores	
Ideas and Content	
Organization	
Voice	
Word Choice	
Sentence Fluency	
Conventions	

Directions: Below write some comments that explain the scores you wrote above. Use specific examples from the text to support your evaluations.

My Comments

Ideas and Content: _____

_____

_____

Organization: _____

_____

_____

Voice: _____

_____

_____

Word Choice: _____

_____

_____

Sentence Fluency: _____

_____

_____

Conventions: _____

_____

_____

Sum It Up: _____

_____

_____

Copyright © 2007 by Holt, Rinehart and Winston. All rights reserved.

Narrative Essay: Read the prompt and the narrative essay below. Then review the Six Trait rubrics on pp. 20–21 and fill in the blank evaluation form that follows.

> **Narrative Prompt:** *Think of an important event or incident that happened to you recently. What lesson did you learn? Write a well-developed personal narrative that describes the experience and reveals why it was important to you.*

The ringing phone jarred me awake.

"Hello," I answered somewhat sternly, wondering who would dare to call me so early on Saturday morning.

"Get up, Maria. We're going to an air show today. Be ready in half an hour."

Before I could even object, Uncle Raul hung up. It's true; Uncle Raul usually took me to interesting events, but an air show? At that moment, sleeping late seemed much more appealing.

Still, I got dressed, ate breakfast, and greeted my uncle thirty minutes later. "This had better be a good show," I warned.

As he drove to the field, he described the Thunderbirds, an elite squadron of Air Force pilots. I listened in silence, too sleepy and grumpy to be excited. When we arrived, I was surprised to see a large number of people standing at the edge of a huge airfield. We finally found a place to stand in the growing crowd.

Six gigantic F-16 jets sat on the runway. The gleaming white bodies of the fighter planes threw off a glare in the hot sun, and I shielded my eyes with my hand. The wings, nose, and tail of each jet were painted with three stripes. The first was red, the next white, and the last one a blue so dark that it looked like the night sky. Over each right wing were the letters USAF.

Just then, an announcement crackled over a loudspeaker. The show was beginning. Six pilots dressed in bright red jumpsuits marched briskly onto the airfield. They climbed into the cockpits and pulled on their shiny helmets. A loud BOOM shook the crowd as the pilots started the jet engines. The pilots then turned to the crowd, gave a thumbs-up sign, and the six jets roared off into the air.

The squadron turned and headed back over the airfield in a diamond formation. Streams of white smoke trailed behind them in the brilliant blue sky. The jets flew so close together that they looked as though their wings were actually touching. They made another pass

Copyright © 2007 by Holt, Rinehart and Winston. All rights reserved.

over us, doing flips and rolls and dives. The announcer called out the names of the maneuvers: "Five Card Loop, Wing Rock-and-Roll, Cuban Eight." Several times I found myself gasping, thinking the jets were about to crash.

Back and forth, up and down, the F-16s roared overhead. Without our noticing it, one jet peeled off from the others. Suddenly it appeared out of nowhere, roaring over our heads. The ground shook. It sounded like a bomb exploding right behind us. We screamed and laughed in relief as the single jet joined the others.

Too soon, the show was over. The Thunderbirds landed, taxied down the runway, and parked. The crowd cheered wildly as the pilots approached, shaking hands, saluting, and signing autographs. I applauded and cheered along with everyone else.

Uncle Raul looked over at me and said, "Well, was this worth getting up for?" I smiled sheepishly. Once again, he gave me experience I would never forget. Never again would I doubt him.

Copyright © 2007 by Holt, Rinehart and Winston. All rights reserved.

Directions: In the table below, write the scores you give the narrative essay for its execution of six writing traits. (The highest score is 5; the lowest is 1.)

Narrative Essay: My Scores	
Ideas and Content	
Organization	
Voice	
Word Choice	
Sentence Fluency	
Conventions	

Directions: Below write some comments that explain the scores you wrote above. Use specific examples from the text to support your evaluations.

My Comments

Ideas and Content: _____
_____
_____

Organization: _____
_____
_____

Voice: _____
_____
_____

Word Choice: _____
_____
_____

Sentence Fluency: _____
_____
_____

Conventions: _____
_____
_____

Sum It Up: _____
_____
_____

Copyright © 2007 by Holt, Rinehart and Winston. All rights reserved.

PART TWO

USING THE SIX TRAITS TO WRITE

WRITING WORKSHOP 1:
Using the Six Traits to Write Expository Text

Remember that your purpose in an expository text is to inform. The main intent is for you to present clear information. Informative writing is used to share knowledge and to convey messages, instructions, and ideas.

PREWRITING The prewriting stage is where you do the work of identifying your purpose and audience, deciding what to write about, drawing upon what you know about the topic, and planning. *Three of the six traits will help you here.*

IDEAS AND CONTENT

- *Explore ideas and choose a topic.*
  Ask questions. Try finding a topic by asking questions about subjects that interest you. (For help, see the brainstorming graphic organizer on p. 89.)

> **Quick Tip!** *In a test situation, a writing prompt will usually give you a specific topic to write about, but you will still need to gather ideas, develop a main idea, and plan.*

- *Gather ideas and details to develop the topic.*
  Look at good sources of information, such as books, magazines, encyclopedias, the internet, and experts in your community.

  Provide logical support for your ideas by using facts, examples, statistics, and expert opinions.

- *Think about your audience and your purpose for writing.*
  Ask "Who am I writing for?" "What do my readers need to know?" "What will they find interesting?" Remember that your purpose is to inform.

ORGANIZATION

- *Develop a thesis or controlling idea.*
  Narrow your topic so that it is not too big. For example, the topic of your three favorite sports is too big. An explanation of the field-goal kick is too narrow. You need something in between, such as how the way football is played has changed over the last ten years.

- *Organize the ideas and details into a coherent structure.*
  Try using order of importance. Start with your least important idea and save the most important idea for last. That way, the reader will remember it better. (For ideas on how to organize your paper, see p. 42.)

VOICE

- *Think about your audience—what voice should you use?*
  Your tone (friendly, calm, stern, neutral) should match your purpose and your topic. A paper about how to make a clown costume can have a friendly, informal voice. A paper about the causes and effects of air pollution needs to be formal, serious. (For help with voice, see p. 8.)

Copyright © 2007 by Holt, Rinehart and Winston. All rights reserved.

WRITING Writing is the stage where you express your main ideas clearly, support those ideas, and follow a plan of organization, adjusting the plan as needed to make meaning clear. *Four of the six traits will help you here.*

 IDEAS AND CONTENT

• *Develop sentences and paragraphs that explain and elaborate on your ideas.*

Each sentence and paragraph should focus on one complete thought or idea.

Provide definitions and background information about your topic.

 **ORGANIZATION**

• *Decide how to introduce the piece effectively.*

Try to grab your readers' attention with an interesting fact or anecdote.

• *State the thesis or controlling idea.*

Make sure your main idea is stated clearly.

• *Organize the piece so that it is coherent.*

As you write, consider the order you decided on in the prewriting stage. If order of importance doesn't work, try chronological order, spatial order, or logical order.

• *Conclude the paper so that it has a sense of closure.*

Don't leave your readers hanging. Review the key ideas and then leave readers with a final thought.

 **VOICE**

• *Include cues that signal tone and make the audience aware of the paper's purpose.*

For example, in a cause-and-effect paper, use words and phrases such as *cause, effect, affect, because, as a result, in the end, so,* and *resulting in.*

WORD CHOICE

• *As you write, use language that effectively conveys your ideas.*

If you use unfamiliar vocabulary, make sure you define the terms and use them properly.

SENTENCE FLUENCY

• *Look at how your sentences flow and connect ideas.*

Include effective transitions between sentences and paragraphs that show the connections between ideas. Vary your sentence constructions, too. Use a mixture of long and short sentences and include sentences that start with phrases or clauses. For a list of effective transitional words and phrases, see p. 105.

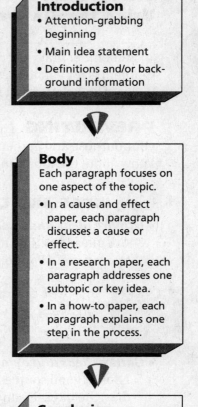

Introduction
• Attention-grabbing beginning
• Main idea statement
• Definitions and/or background information

Body
Each paragraph focuses on one aspect of the topic.
• In a cause and effect paper, each paragraph discusses a cause or effect.
• In a research paper, each paragraph addresses one subtopic or key idea.
• In a how-to paper, each paragraph explains one step in the process.

Conclusion
• Summary of ideas
• Restatement of main idea
• Additional insight into the topic

Copyright © 2007 by Holt, Rinehart and Winston. All rights reserved.

REVISING AND EVALUATING
The revising and evaluating stage may be the most important in the process of writing an informative paper. It is where you figure out if your ideas, organization, and style are working and that you are communicating your ideas clearly. *Five of the six traits will help you here.*

IDEAS AND CONTENT

- *Evaluate and revise the ideas and content of the paper.*
  Do all your ideas and details "fit" the paper and support your main idea? Use the Content and Organization Guidelines for Self-Evaluation and Peer Evaluation below. They will help you decide if you need to edit or revise any of your ideas and content.

Quick Tip!

Definition: Edit or Revise? Many people use the words edit and revise interchangeably. Dictionaries define edit as "to revise and make a text ready for publication." They define revise as "to correct and improve a text." Follow your teacher's guidance here.

ORGANIZATION

- *Evaluate and revise the organization of the paper.*
  Have you placed your ideas in a way that makes sense to the reader and suits the topic? Use the Content and Organization Guidelines for Self-Evaluation and Peer Evaluation below. They will help you decide if you need to change your organizational structure.

VOICE

- *Refine the style of the paper so that it suits the audience and purpose and conveys the appropriate voice.*
  Your voice lets readers know what you think about your topic and your audience. Are you friendly or formal, concerned or indifferent? Let readers know through your tone and style. (See p. 8 in this book for help with voice.)

Quick Tip!

Style Guideline - Passive and Active Voice

Passive voice expresses an action done to the subject.	Active voice expresses an action done by the subject.
The tree was knocked over by the wind.	*The wind knocked over the tree.*

Use active voice as much as possible. It makes your writing clearer and more direct. To identify passive voice, look for forms of be used as helping verbs.

WORD CHOICE

- *Evaluate and revise the words you use.*
  Your choice of words should reflect your attitude toward your subject and audience. Think about the connotations of the words you use in your writing. (See pp. 11–13 for help with word choice.)

Copyright © 2007 by Holt, Rinehart and Winston. All rights reserved.

SENTENCE FLUENCY

- *Evaluate and revise the way you connect ideas in your sentences and paragraphs.*

    You may think the connections between your ideas are obvious, but you know your material better than the reader does. Use transitional words and phrases to show those connections. Also, make sure some of your sentences start with phrases or clauses, to make your writing more interesting. (Also, see pp. 14–16 for help with sentence fluency.)

The guidelines below offer questions, tips, and techniques that will help you edit and revise your writing.

Content and Organization Guidelines for Self-Evaluation and Peer Evaluation

Evaluation Questions	Tip	Editing/Revision Techniques
1. Does the introduction include a clear main idea statement? Does the paper have a conclusion that summarizes the main points and closes with an interesting observation?	**Underline** the main idea. Ask whether it identifies a clear and interesting idea. **Draw a box** around the conclusion. Ask if it accurately reflects the content of your paper and includes an interesting observation.	**Add** a clear statement of main idea if one is missing. If the conclusion does not summarize your main points, **add** a summary. If it does not have an interesting observation, **add** one.
2. Does each paragraph discuss or focus on one idea? Does the support flow logically from one idea to the next?	Put a **check** by each idea in a paragraph. Put an **asterisk** next to each supporting detail.	**Rearrange** the ideas and support so that each paragraph contains one idea and its supporting evidence.
3. Is the tone of the paper appropriate for the audience?	In the margins, **write** an adjective that describes the tone of voice in each paragraph.	If the tone changes abruptly or does not match the content or the audience, **adjust** word choice and phrasing to make it more appropriate.
4. Do you use words that help readers understand your ideas? Do you use helpful cue words or phrases? Do your words add life to your writing?	**Circle** all the cue words or phrases in a paragraph. **Draw boxes** around words or phrases that add "flavor" to your writing.	If a paragraph has no circled words, reread it and see where you can **add** cue words or phrases. If no words are boxed, consult a thesaurus to find synonyms that have more flavor.
5. Do transitions help flow ideas together coherently?	**Mark** transitional words or phrases **with stars.**	**Add** transitional words or phrases if needed.

Copyright © 2007 by Holt, Rinehart and Winston. All rights reserved.

PUBLISHING Publishing is the stage in the writing process where you make your paper ready for your actual readers. *As you prepare your paper for publication, consider four of the six traits.*

IDEAS AND CONTENT

- *Reflect on your completed paper.*

   Consider how you might approach a similar writing assignment next time. Ask yourself the following questions:

   - How well did I achieve the purpose of sharing information with my audience?
   - Which part of my final draft was most effective? Which was the least?
   - The part of writing an informative paper that I liked most/least was...?

VOICE

- *Publish your paper for its intended audience.*

   Think about the tone and attitude you convey in your paper. Ask yourself if the voice you used really suited both your topic and your audience.

SENTENCE FLUENCY

- *Identify and correct errors in sentence construction.*

   This is your last chance to fix any simple errors in your sentence constructions. For example, have you used the same verb tense consistently throughout your paper? The Proofreading Guidelines and the Grammar Links that appear throughout Elements of Language will help you with sentence construction errors. Also, see pp. 00–00 for help with sentence fluency problems.

CONVENTIONS

- *Proofread and edit the paper to catch and correct errors in paragraphing, spelling, capitalization, punctuation and grammar.*

   Look in Elements of Language for help with specific kinds of errors. Also, see the conventional errors checklist on p. 000.

ONE MORE TRAIT: PRESENTATION/PUBLICATION

There is one more trait to consider when writing a paper—presentation and publication. A published paper should have a clean, pleasant appearance and should not contain visual elements that may distract the reader. Use the checklist below to make sure that your paper looks its best

---

√ If handwritten, your letters are consistently and clearly formed, spacing is reasonable and uniform, and the words are easy to see and read.

√ If typed or word-processed, your letters and words appear in a font and size that is easy to read.

√ There is a balance of white space (margins, spaces between words and paragraphs) and text on the page that allows the reader to focus on the text.

√ Any titles, subheadings, page numbers, bullets, and other graphics are the appropriate size and boldness. They help readers follow the flow of ideas. They do not distract readers from the words or the message of the text.

Copyright © 2007 by Holt, Rinehart and Winston. All rights reserved.

WRITING WORKSHOP 2:
Using the Six Traits to Write Persuasive Text

Remember that your purpose is to persuade. The main intent is for you to state a clear opinion and support it with convincing evidence. Persuasive writing is used to share opinions and to influence readers' thoughts, opinions, feelings, and actions.

PREWRITING Prewriting is the stage in which you choose an interesting issue and determine your opinion. *Three of the six traits will help you here.*

IDEAS AND CONTENT

• *Explore ideas and choose an issue.*

Look around you. Remember that an issue is a subject about which people disagree. Read newspapers and talk to family and friends.

When you think you have found a good issue, ask yourself these questions:
- Is the issue debatable? Will people disagree about it?
- Do I have strong feelings about the issue?
- Would other people have strong feelings?

> **Quick Tip!** *In a test situation, a persuasive writing prompt may provide you with an issue and even an opinion to argue. You may not care deeply about the issue, but you must write persuasively. Use your brains, not your heart. Think of as much evidence as you can and present it in a logical way.*

• *State your opinion.*

An opinion statement—which will be your thesis statement or main idea—is a statement that tells both the issue and your point of view. It lets readers know where you stand.

• *Think about your audience.*

Ask "What type of people will read my paper?" "How do they probably feel about the issue?" "What objections might they have to my ideas?"

• *Evaluate and support reasons.*

Do some research. Make sure that there are good reasons and solid evidence to support your opinion. Reasons tell why you have a particular point of view. Evidence includes facts, statistics, examples, anecdotes, and expert opinions. Evidence backs up your claim and makes it credible or believable.

ORGANIZATION

• *Organize the ideas and details logically.*

Effective persuasive writing is usually organized in a logical way. Think of at least three reasons to support your opinion. Then support each reason with evidence. Group your ideas logically. Try order of importance. (For ideas on how to organize your persuasive paper, see p. 91.)

VOICE

• *Think about the tone should you use.*

Writers who want to appeal to their readers' sense reason, use a voice that is serious, formal, and polite. (For help with voice, see p. 8.)

Copyright © 2007 by Holt, Rinehart and Winston. All rights reserved.

WRITING The writing stage is where you put your ideas down on paper. *Four of the six traits will help you with writing your persuasive paper.*

IDEAS AND CONTENT

- *Develop sentences and paragraphs that identify your opinion and support it with persuasive evidence.*

  Make sure you have enough to talk about. Each reason should have at least one piece of evidence to support it.

ORGANIZATION

- *Grab readers' attention by appealing to their self-interest.*

  First, identify the issue in an interesting way. Then tell readers how the issue affects them every day.

- *State your opinion up front.*

  Tell your readers exactly what you think about the issue in the introduction.

- *Use logical appeal.*

  Order of importance works best in persuasive papers. Dedicate at least one paragraph to each of your reasons. Support the reasons with evidence. Elaborate on the evidence so that readers understand exactly what you mean.

- *Conclude the paper with a call to action.*

  Restate your opinion and your reasons. Then close with a call to action—tell readers what you want them to do or think.

VOICE

- *Use your voice to convey the importance of the issue.*

  Make sure your voice reflects the seriousness of the topic. Also, even if your readers disagree with your opinion, they deserve your respect. Use a voice that conveys respect and intelligence. Consider using the first-person.

WORD CHOICE

- *As you write, use language that effectively conveys your ideas.*

  Choose words that accurately describe the issue. If you must use jargon or technical terms, define them.

SENTENCE FLUENCY

- *Make clear transitions between ideas.*

  You want your readers to follow your argument, so use clear transitional words and phrases to help them keep up with you. (For a list of effective transitional words and phrases, see p. 105.) Also, don't show off with lots of long, complicated sentences. Use sentences that are clear and succinct.

Introduction
- Attention-grabbing beginning
- Opinion statement

▼

Body
- Reason #1
- Evidence and elaboration
- Reason #2
- Evidence and elaboration and so on.

▼

Conclusion
- Restatement of opinion
- Summary of reasons
- Call to action or closing statement

Copyright © 2007 by Holt, Rinehart and Winston. All rights reserved.

REVISING AND EVALUATING
The revising and evaluating stage is the most important in the process of writing a persuasive paper. It is where you figure out if your ideas, organization, and style are working and that you are communicating your ideas clearly. *Five of the six traits will help you here.*

IDEAS AND CONTENT
- *Evaluate and revise your opinion and evidence.*

   Is your opinion reasonable? Is it adequately supported by your reasons and evidence? Use the Content and Organization Guidelines for Self-Evaluation and Peer Evaluation. They will help you decide if you need to edit or revise any of your ideas and content.

ORGANIZATION
- *Evaluate and revise the organization of the paper.*

   Have you organized your argument in a way that makes sense to the reader and suits the issue? Use the Content and Organization Guidelines for Self-Evaluation and Peer Evaluation. They will help you decide if you need to change your organizational structure.

VOICE
- *Refine the style of the paper so that it suits the audience and purpose and conveys the appropriate voice.*

   Your voice lets readers know what you think about your topic and your audience. Are you friendly or formal, concerned or indifferent? Let readers know through your tone and style. (See pp. 8–10 in this book for help with voice.)

> **Quick Tip!**
>
> *Style Guideline - Emotional Appeal*
> *Emotional appeal is another persuasive tactic. It involves using language and ideas that appeal to readers' feelings rather than to their intellect. It is a powerful technique but can easily backfire. It relies on the writer's voice more than on evidence. In testing situations, it is best to stick with logical appeal.*

WORD CHOICE
- *Evaluate and revise the words you use.*

   Your choice of words should reflect your attitude toward the issue and your audience. As you revise, make sure that you have not used loaded language. Make sure you know the connotations of the words you use. (Also see pp. 11–13 for help with word choice.)

SENTENCE FLUENCY
- *Evaluate and revise the way you connect ideas in your sentences and paragraphs.*

   Make sure your transitional words and phrases are clear. Also, make sure some of your sentences start with phrases or clauses, to make your writing more interesting. (Also, see pp. 14–16 for help with sentence fluency.)

Copyright © 2007 by Holt, Rinehart and Winston. All rights reserved.

The guidelines below offer questions, tips, and techniques that will help you edit and revise your persuasive writing.

Content and Organization Guidelines for Self-Evaluation and Peer Evaluation

Evaluation Questions	Tip	Editing/Revision Techniques
1. Does the introduction include a clear opinion statement? Does the conclusion restate the opinion and reasons and have a call to action?	**Underline** the opinion. Ask whether it expresses a point of view. **Draw a box** around the conclusion. Make sure it restates the opinion and includes a call to action.	**Add** a clear opinion if one is missing. If the conclusion does not summarize your reasons, **add** a summary. If it does not have an call to action, add one.
2. Do the paragraphs progress in order of importance? Does the writer give reasons to support the opinion? Are the reasons supported by evidence?	**Number** the paragraphs in order of importance. **Put a star** next to each reason and **highlight** the evidence for each reason.	**Rearrange** the order of paragraphs, if necessary. **Add** a reason, or **add** a fact, statistic, anecdote, example, or expert opinion to support a reason, if necessary.
3. Is the tone of the paper appropriate for the audience?	In the margins, **write** an adjective that describes the tone of voice in each paragraph.	If the tone changes abruptly or does not match the content or the audience, **adjust** the language to make it more appropriate.
4. Do you use opinion words that help readers understand your point of view? Do your words add spice to your writing?	**Circle** all the opinion words or phrases in a paragraph. **Draw boxes** around words or phrases that you think add "flavor" to your writing.	If a paragraph has no circled words, reread it and see where you can **add** opinion words or phrases. If no words are boxed, **consult** a thesaurus to find synonyms that have more flavor.
5. Do transitions help flow ideas together logically and coherently?	**Mark** transitional words or phrases **with stars.**	**Add** transitional words or phrases if needed.

Copyright © 2007 by Holt, Rinehart and Winston. All rights reserved.

PUBLISHING Publishing is the stage in the writing process where you make your paper ready for your actual readers. *As you prepare your paper for publication, consider four of the six traits.*

IDEAS AND CONTENT

- *Reflect on your completed paper.*

    Consider how you might approach a similar writing assignment next time. Ask yourself the following questions:
    - Did I feel that my opinion statement was really strong and convincing? Why or why not?
    - Which piece of evidence in my paper was strongest? Which was the weakest?
    - How difficult was it to find supporting evidence? Will it be easier next time?
    - Could my writing have been more convincing? Why or why not?

VOICE

- *Publish your paper for its intended audience.*

    How would you describe your voice? Think about the tone and attitude you convey in your paper. Ask yourself if the voice you used really suited both your issue and your audience.

SENTENCE FLUENCY

- *Identify and correct errors in sentence construction.*

    This is your last chance to fix any simple sentence construction problems in your paper. For example, have you used the same subject-verb-object construction in every sentence? You might change a few sentences for variety's sake. Also, see pp. 14–16 for help with sentence fluency problems.

CONVENTIONS

- *Proofread and edit the paper to catch and correct errors in paragraphing, spelling, capitalization, punctuation and grammar.*

    Also, see the conventional errors checklist on p. 106.

ONE MORE TRAIT: PRESENTATION/PUBLICATION

Your published paper should have a clean, pleasant appearance and should not contain visual elements that may distract the reader. Use the checklist below to make sure that your paper looks its best.

√ If handwritten, your letters are consistently and clearly formed, spacing is reasonable and uniform, and the words are easy to see and read.

√ If typed or word-processed, your letters and words appear in a font and size that is easy to read.

√ There is a balance of white space (margins, spaces between words and paragraphs) and text on the page that allows the reader to focus on the text.

√ Any titles, subheadings, page numbers, bullets, and other graphics are the appropriate size and boldness. They help readers follow the flow of ideas. They do not distract readers from the words or the message of the text.

Copyright © 2007 by Holt, Rinehart and Winston. All rights reserved.

WRITING WORKSHOP 3:
Using the Six Traits to Write Narrative Text

Remember that your purpose is to tell a story. You will retell the events in the order they took place using interesting characters, images, and dialogue. The narrative should have an implied main idea or express a theme—an idea about the human condition.

PREWRITING Prewriting is where you do the work of choosing an experience or event to retell. *Three of the six traits will help you here.*

IDEAS AND CONTENT

- *Explore ideas and choose an event.*

    Personal narratives are stories from your past. Historical narratives or eyewitness accounts retell historical or recent events. If you are writing about your own past, reread at old journal entries or look in photo albums. If you are writing about history, think about past events or heroes that interest you. (For help, see the brainstorming graphic organizer on p. 89.)

Quick Tip! *Narrative writing prompts often require you to write a personal narrative. They may ask you to write about an experience in which you learned or felt something. Choose an experience that is meaningful and isn't too personal.*

- *Evaluate your ideas.*

    Ask yourself some questions: "Will readers find this story interesting?" "Can I tell it neatly and convey its importance?" "If it's a personal experience, do I mind sharing it with others?"

- *Think about your audience and your purpose for writing.*

    In a personal narrative, your main purpose is to express yourself by telling about a something that happened to you. Your audience will expect you to write in the first person, to tell events in order, and to reveal your feelings. Can your audience handle it? If not, change your topic.

ORGANIZATION

- *Create a time line.*

    Most personal narratives are told in chronological order, the order in which events took place. Sometimes, though, flashbacks are fun. They start the story in the middle and "flash back" in time to show the background. (For ideas on how to organize your paper, see p. 52.)

VOICE

- *Think about your audience—what voice should you use?*

    You get to express your individual voice in a personal narrative. Use a voice that suits your narrative. For example, if you are writing about something that happened when you were four, you might use the voice of a young child. For historical narratives or eyewitness accounts, a serious, formal voice is best. (For help with voice, see p. 8.)

Copyright © 2007 by Holt, Rinehart and Winston. All rights reserved.

WRITING Writing is the part where you put your ideas down on paper. *Four of the six traits will help you here.*

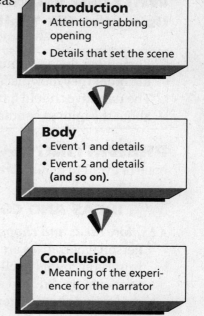

Introduction
- Attention-grabbing opening
- Details that set the scene

Body
- Event 1 and details
- Event 2 and details **(and so on).**

Conclusion
- Meaning of the experience for the narrator

IDEAS AND CONTENT

- *Frame your event.*

   Think about where your narrative will begin and where it will end. As you write, also think about the point of the story. Every narrative says something, either directly or indirectly, about the writer or the world. Make sure the details in the middle tell an interesting story.

ORGANIZATION

- *Tell events in the order they happened.*

   Use chronological order to tell your story. You can jazz things up by using flashbacks or build suspense by using a flash-forward (telling about events to come), but use these techniques only if they enhance the telling of the narrative. Be sure to set the scene and establish the "characters" early on in the narrative. Make sure the meaning of the experience gets expressed.

VOICE

- *Make sure your voice rings loud and clear.*

   Create a voice that sounds natural for the "character" that you are in a personal narrative. If you are young and naïve, your voice should reflect that. If you are a cynical teen, again your voice should reflect those qualities. Personal narratives are one form of writing that really lets a writer discover his or her own voice.

WORD CHOICE

- *As you write, choose language that best reflects your characters.*

   Narratives allow writers to use dialogue that lets characters speak directly to the readers and in their own words. Feel free to use slang, informal language, and jargon—if that is what your narrator and characters would use. In descriptive passages, use words that really capture the scene. Appeal to your readers' five senses.

SENTENCE FLUENCY

- *Play with sentence length and even break the rules.*

   In narratives, writers often use sentence fragments to convey what real speech sounds like. Experiment with sentence fragments in your narrative. See how they affect your style and rhythm of writing. Ultimately, though, follow your teacher's guidance about the use of fragments.

Copyright © 2007 by Holt, Rinehart and Winston. All rights reserved.

REVISING AND EVALUATING
The revising and evaluating stage is the most important in the process of writing a narrative paper. It is where you figure out if your ideas, organization, and style are working and that you are communicating your ideas clearly. *Five of the six traits will help you here.*

IDEAS AND CONTENT

• *Evaluate and revise the ideas and content of the paper. Have you told too much?* Can you focus on the most important events in the narrative and trim out a few? What key idea do you express in the narrative? Is it clear? Use the Content and Organization Guidelines for Self-Evaluation and Peer Evaluation on the next page. They will help you decide if you need to edit or revise any of your ideas and content.

ORGANIZATION

• *Evaluate and revise the organization of the paper.* Have you told events in a logical order? Use the Content and Organization Guidelines for Self-Evaluation and Peer Evaluation on the next page. They will help you decide if you need to change your organizational structure.

VOICE

• *Refine the style of the paper so that it suits the audience and purpose and conveys the appropriate voice.* Does your voice engage readers and sound "real"? (Also, see pp. 8–10 in this book for help with voice.)

WORD CHOICE

• *Evaluate and revise the words you use.* Your choice of words should make the narrative come alive and make the voice or voices sound real. Read your narrative aloud to see how the dialogue sounds. (Also see pp. 11–13 for help with word choice.)

SENTENCE FLUENCY

• *Evaluate and revise your sentences and paragraphs.* In narrative writing, paragraphs are often shorter and interrupted by dialogue. Make sure that you are breaking sentences and paragraphs correctly and that your sentences are natural sounding. (Also, see pp. 14–16 for help with sentence fluency.)

Quick Tip!

Style Guideline – Sentence Lengths
Variety in sentence length adds rhythm and style. Short, choppy sentences suggest a breathless, suspenseful situation. Long sentences suggest the writer is in complete control. Using both lengths gives rhythm to your writing.

Short and choppy: *The doorbell rang. I answered the door. No one was there! I felt a little freaked out. (Do you feel the writer's tension?)*

Combined: *The doorbell rang and I answered the door, but when no one was there, I felt a little freaked out. (Does the writer really sound scared?)*

Copyright © 2007 by Holt, Rinehart and Winston. All rights reserved.

The guidelines below offer questions, tips, and techniques that will help you edit and revise your persuasive writing.

Content and Organization Guidelines
for Self-Evaluation and Peer Evaluation

Evaluation Questions	Tip	Editing/Revision Techniques
1. Does the beginning grab the audience's attention and set the scene? Does the narrative convey an important message at the end?	**Put stars** next to quotations, surprising details, or statements that would interest the audience. **Circle** details that show when and where the experience happened. **Underline** the writer's statement of why the experience is meaningful.	If needed, **add** a quotation, surprising detail, or interesting statement. **Add** details about when and where the event happened. **Add** a statement that explains the narrative's importance, if necessary.
2. Are the events in chronological order?	**Number** the events as they appear in the paper. Compare the numbered events to the actual order of events.	**Rearrange** the order of events, if necessary.
3. Is the voice in the paper appropriate for the story and the audience?	In the margins, **write** an adjective that describes the voice in the story.	If the tone changes abruptly or does not match the content or the audience, **adjust** word choice and phrasing to make it more appropriate.
4. Do the words used by the narrator and any characters in the narrative sound "true"?	**Circle** all the words or phrases that you think sound "true" to the narrator or characters' voices.	If a paragraph has no circled words, **reread** it and see where you can **add** words or phrases that sound natural. **Consult** a thesaurus to find synonyms that have more flavor.
5. Do the sentences lengths create a sense of rhythm and style? Do they convey the writer's emotions?	**Place stars** next to sentences that really create rhythm or style. **Write** the emotion they help convey in the margin.	**Adjust** sentence lengths to create a certain rhythm, emotion, or style.

Copyright © 2007 by Holt, Rinehart and Winston. All rights reserved.

PUBLISHING Publishing is the stage in the writing process where you make your paper ready for your actual readers. *As you prepare your paper for publication, consider four of the six traits.*

IDEAS AND CONTENT

- *Reflect on your completed paper.*
  Consider how you might approach a similar writing assignment next time. Ask yourself the following questions:

  - What was the clearest or most exciting detail in my narrative? Why do I think so?
  - Was I able to find meaning in my experience as I wrote about it?
  - What was the hardest part of writing the narrative—setting the scene? writing the dialogue? creating style with my sentences?

VOICE

- *Publish your paper for its intended audience.*
  How would you describe your voice in your narrative? Ask yourself if were able to create the voice you wanted.

SENTENCE FLUENCY

- *Identify and correct errors in sentence construction.*
  This is your last chance to fix any simple sentence construction problems in your paper. For example, you might double-check that you have not used included any run-on or stringy sentences in your narrative. Also, see pp. 14–16 for help with sentence fluency problems.

CONVENTIONS

- *Proofread and edit the paper to catch and correct errors in paragraphing, spelling, capitalization, punctuation and grammar.*
  See the conventional errors checklist on p. 17.

ONE MORE TRAIT: PRESENTATION/PUBLICATION

Your published paper should have a clean, pleasant appearance and should not contain visual elements that may distract the reader. Use the checklist below to make sure that your paper looks its best.

√ If handwritten, your letters are consistently and clearly formed, spacing is reasonable and uniform, and the words are easy to see and read.

√ If typed or word-processed, your letters and words appear in a font and size that is easy to read.

√ There is a balance of white space (margins, spaces between words and paragraphs) and text on the page that allows the reader to focus on the text.

√ Any titles, subheadings, page numbers, bullets, and other graphics are the appropriate size and boldness. They help readers follow the flow of ideas. They do not distract readers from the words or the message of the text.

Copyright © 2007 by Holt, Rinehart and Winston. All rights reserved.

The following chart shows how to integrate the instruction and features in *Elements of Language* and the Six Traits.

At-a-Glance: The Six Traits of Writing and the Writing Process

SIX TRAITS	Elements of Language			
	Prewriting	Writing	Revising and Editing	Publishing (Proofreading and editing)
Ideas and Content	Explore ideas and choose a topic Gather ideas and details to develop the topic Evaluate ideas using **Writing** or **Critical-Thinking Mini-Lessons**	Develop sentences and paragraphs that explain and elaborate on the writer's ideas, referring to the **Framework** and **A Writer's Model** for suggestions and examples	Evaluate and revise the content of the piece using Content and **Organization Guidelines for Peer and Self-Evaluation**	Reflect on the completed piece. Consider, for example, how to approach a similar piece next time
Organization	Develop a thesis, opinion statement, or controlling idea Organize the ideas and details into a coherent structure	Decide how to introduce the piece effectively State the thesis or controlling idea Organize the piece so that it is coherent, referring to the **Framework** for directions and explanations Conclude the piece so that it has a sense of closure	Evaluate and revise the organization of the piece using **Content and Organization Guidelines for Peer and Self-Evaluation**	
Voice	Think about audience, purpose and tone, using **Thinking It Through** and **Writing** or **Critical Thinking Mini-Lessons**	Include cues that signal tone and make the audience aware of the piece's purpose	Use **Style Guidelines** to refine the style of the piece so that it suits the audience and purpose and conveys the writer's voice	Publish the piece for its intended audience

Copyright © 2007 by Holt, Rinehart and Winston. All rights reserved.

SIX TRAITS	Elements of Language			
	Prewriting	**Writing**	**Revising and Editing**	**Publishing (Proofreading and editing)**
Word Choice		Refer to **A Writer's Model** for examples of using language effectively to convey ideas	Evaluate and revise the style of piece in **Style Guidelines** or **Focus on Word Choice**	
Sentence Fluency		Use suggestions in **Framework** to build effective transitions between sentences	Evaluate and revise the style of piece in **Style Guidelines** or **Focus on Sentences**	Use **Proofreading Guidelines** to identify and correct errors in sentence construction
Conventions				Proofread the piece to catch and correct errors in spelling, capitalization, punctuation and grammar—using **Guidelines for Proofreading** and the instruction and practice in **Grammar Link**
One More Trait: Presentation/ Publishing				Determine how to share the piece with the intended audience Format the piece for presentation using suggestions in **Designing Your Writing**

Copyright © 2007 by Holt, Rinehart and Winston. All rights reserved.

PART THREE

WRITING PROMPTS

HOW TO READ AND ANALYZE A WRITING PROMPT

A prompt is a writing assignment. Most state tests include writing prompts. Most prompts provide you with a topic for writing and give some specific suggestions for how get started. They will usually identify the type of writing you are to do and the audience for which you should write. The formats of writing prompts will vary. Prompts may ask questions, tell you to respond to a quotation, challenge you with an opinion, or set up a hypothetical situation.

Here is an example of a persuasive writing prompt.

> *Your state is considering new policy that would require a young person to have a high school diploma before he or she can apply for a driver's license. What do you think? Write a letter to the editor of your local newspaper stating your opinion and supporting it with convincing reasons.*

Steps for Reading and Analyzing a Prompt

STEP 1 **Read the prompt once or twice. Then determine your audience.** Who is your reader? If your audience is not stated directly, assume that it is the general adult population.

STEP 2 **Decide on your topic.** What is the key idea or opinion that the prompt wants you to discuss?

STEP 3 **Look for cue words.** Not every prompt will have a label telling what kind of writing is expected. Look for words that indicate your task or purpose. (See the chart below.)

Type of Prompt	Cue Words	Task or Purpose
Informational	*explain what, how, or why*	Give facts, ideas, or other kinds of information on a topic, or explain how to do something.
Persuasive	*convince, persuade, or defend*	Take a point of view on an issue, and provide reasons and evidence that support your opinion.
Narrative	*tell, retell, recall, or remember*	Tell about or recall a meaningful event. Include interesting and specific details, dialogue, and characters to express your ideas.

STEP 4 **Identify your task or purpose for writing.** How will you address the topic in your response? Does the prompt tell you to write an essay or another form of writing (like a letter)?

Once you figure out who your audience is and what your topic and purpose for writing are, you can use the writing process (prewriting, writing, revising, and publishing) and the six traits to prepare and polish your response.

Copyright © 2007 by Holt, Rinehart and Winston. All rights reserved.

Expository Writing Prompts for Practice

Remember, **informational, or expository, writing prompts will ask you to explain something.** Use the writing process and the six traits to prepare responses to these prompts. Write your responses on your own paper. Use the rubrics on pp. 20–21 to evaluate your responses.

Practice Prompt 1:

Most people have a favorite season of the year. Think about which season you like best. Then explain in an essay why this season is your favorite. Be sure to use sensory details to support your response.

Practice Prompt 2:

Some teachers grade students on class participation. Write an essay in which you explain both what is good and what is bad about grading for class participation. Be sure to explain each point fully and to be balanced in your discussion.

Practice Prompt 3:

Think of something you have succeeded doing—an accomplishment, a goal you met, or a dream you realized. Then explain how you reached your success. Describe each step in the process, including setbacks and lucky breaks. Finally, tell readers what you learned from the experience.

Copyright © 2007 by Holt, Rinehart and Winston. All rights reserved.

Practice Prompt 4:

Think about the qualities of a successful person—a professional athlete, a world-class musician, a fine writer, or a scientist who makes a world-changing discovery. What do you think causes, or inspires, people to be great? In an essay, talk about the causes or effects of greatness. The effects may be positive, negative, or both. Use examples from real life, books, movies, and television.

Practice Prompt 5:

The United States has been described as a "great melting pot" in which people of all backgrounds come together and are blended into a single, democratic society. Write an essay in which you explain how American society is or is not like a melting pot today. You may use examples from real life as well as from books, movies, or television shows.

Practice Prompt 6:

In his second inaugural address in 1937, President Franklin D. Roosevelt addressed a nation that was still experiencing widespread economic depression. He said, "The test of our progress is not whether we add more to the abundance of those who have much; it is whether we provide enough for those who have too little." Write an essay that explains what Roosevelt meant in this quotation. You may use examples from real life, books, movies, or television.

Copyright © 2007 by Holt, Rinehart and Winston. All rights reserved.

Persuasive Writing Prompts for Practice

Remember, persuasive writing prompts will ask you to state an opinion about an issue and support it with strong reasons. Use the writing process and the six traits to prepare responses to these prompts. Write your responses on your own paper. Use the rubrics on pp. 20–21 to evaluate your responses.

Practice Prompt 1:

Your school district is considering changing school hours so that classes begin and end an hour earlier. Instead of arriving at school at 8:30 and leaving at 2:45, students would attend school from 7:30 to 1:45. Write an essay in which you state an opinion about this change and provide reasons that support your opinion.

Practice Prompt 2:

Are dress codes a restriction on personal freedom? Do dress codes at school help maintain discipline and reduce distractions? Write a well-organized paper in which you state and give reasons for your opinion on this issue.

Practice Prompt 3:

The local public library wants to shut down every weekday afternoon in order to discourage middle- and high-school students from using the library. Librarians say that the students are noisy and disruptive and use the library only because they have nowhere else to go after school. Should the library be able to close its doors to young people? Write an essay in which you state and give reasons and details for your opinion.

Copyright © 2007 by Holt, Rinehart and Winston. All rights reserved.

(Persuasive Writing Prompts continued)

Practice Prompt 4:

A local business will pay for expensive sports equipment for your school. In return, the school must place ads for the business around the school—in the gymnasium, on the sides of school buses, and in the cafeteria. What is your opinion about this trade-off? Write an essay in which you state an opinion and give reasons to support it.

Practice Prompt 5:

Read the quotation below from Roman historian Gaius Sallustius Crispus (c. 86–35/34 B.C.).

> *"The fame which is based on wealth or beauty is a frail and fleeting thing; but virtue shines for ages with undiminished luster."*

Do you agree or disagree with Crispus' thoughts on fame? Write a persuasive essay in which you support or challenge his point of view and give reasons that back up your opinion. Use examples from real life, literature, and the media.

Practice Prompt 6:

Think about current events and world issues you have learned about recently. Examples might include global warming, the war on terrorism, the world's continuing need for resources such as oil and clean water. Which issue do you think is the most pressing—the one you will continue to deal with as you become an adult? Write an essay in which you identify the issue and express an opinion about it. Give reasons that support your opinion and use examples from real life, literature, and the media.

Copyright © 2007 by Holt, Rinehart and Winston. All rights reserved.

Narrative Writing Prompts for Practice

Remember, narrative writing prompts will ask you to tell a story or recall an experience. Use the writing process and the six traits to prepare responses to these prompts. Write your responses on your own paper. Use the rubrics on pp. 20–21 to evaluate your responses.

Practice Prompt 1:

Think of an important event or incident in your life. What lesson did you learn from it? Write a well-developed personal narrative that describes the experience and reveals why it was important to you. Select an event that you feel comfortable sharing with readers.

Practice Prompt 2:

Think of a story that has often been retold by your family members or friends. Why is the story so well loved? What does the story reveal about the people in who tell it? Retell the story in your own words and make sure that the story's significance to your family or friends is clear. Select a story that you feel comfortable sharing with readers.

Practice Prompt 3:

Recall a time in your life when you felt your loyalty was being tested. What was that experience like? Write a well-developed personal essay in which you describe the experience and reveal what you learned about yourself and the people in your life. Select an event that you feel comfortable sharing with readers.

Copyright © 2007 by Holt, Rinehart and Winston. All rights reserved.

Practice Prompt 4:

Life is full of "firsts"—the first time you went swimming, the first time you took the bus by yourself, the first time you tasted your favorite food. Select a "first" that was important. In a well-written personal narrative, describe the events around your experience. Make sure your narrative makes clear why the event was important or significant. Choose an event you won't mind others reading about.

Practice Prompt 5:

Adolescence is a time when young people start to realize that they are unique. How are you unique? Think of an episode from your life in which you realized that you were different from those around you. In a well-written personal narrative, retell the events of that episode. Use dialogue and details to make the experience come alive for readers. Make sure your readers understand what you learned from the experience. Choose an experience you feel comfortable sharing with others.

Practice Prompt 6:

Whom do you admire? Think of a person in your life who inspires you to be great. Select an event from that person's life that shows why you think he or she is admirable. In a well-written narrative, describe the episode or event. Make sure that your readers understand why you admire your subject so much. Make sure the person you write about does not mind if you share details about his or her life.

Copyright © 2007 by Holt, Rinehart and Winston. All rights reserved.

PART FOUR:

RUBRICS, SUPPORT MATERIALS, AND WORKSHEETS

TEACHER/EVALUATOR

SIX TRAITS RUBRIC: IDEAS AND CONTENT

Score 5	It's Crystal Clear!
A Score 5 paper is clear, focused, and interesting. It presents relevant and concrete details that catch and maintain the reader's interest and support a clear main idea, theme, or story line.	√ The topic is clearly focused—neither too broad nor too narrow—for a paper of its kind. √ The ideas are original, interesting, and creative. √ The writer draws from personal experience or knowledge. √ Key details are insightful and well chosen; they are not obvious, predictable, or clichéd. √ The development of the topic is thorough and logical; the writer anticipates and answers the reader's questions. √ Supporting details are accurate and relevant; every detail contributes to the whole.
Score 3	**Close—It's Getting There**
A Score 3 paper develops the topic in a general or basic way; although clear, the ideas in the paper are routine and lack insight.	√ The topic is underdeveloped, but readers can still understand the writer's purpose and predict how ideas will develop. √ Supporting details are present but can be vague and do not help illustrate the main idea or theme; the writer refers to his or her own experience or knowledge but often fails to push beyond the obvious to more specific ideas. √ Ideas are understandable but not detailed, elaborated upon, or personalized; the writer's ideas do not reveal deep comprehension of the topic or of the writing task. √ The writer does not stray from the topic, but the ideas remain general, forcing readers to rely on what they already know to make sense of the paper; more information is needed to create a complete picture.
Score 1	**Hmm. What Is the Writer Trying to Say?**
A Score 1 paper fails to exhibit any clear purpose or main idea. The reader must infer a coherent and meaningful message from scattered details and incomplete observations.	√ The writer appears not to have decided on a topic or main idea; the paper reads like rough draft or brainstorming notes; it is full of random thoughts. √ The thesis is a vague statement about the topic or a restatement of a prompt, with little or no support, detail, or insight. √ Information is limited and spotty; readers must make inferences to make connections or to identify any organizational pattern. √ The text is rambling and repetitious; ideas are underdeveloped; the paper is too short. √ The paper lacks subordination of ideas; every idea and detail seems equally weighted; ideas are not tied to an overarching thesis or theme.

Copyright © 2007 by Holt, Rinehart and Winston. All rights reserved.

SIX TRAITS RUBRIC: ORGANIZATION

Score 5	Yes! I Can See Where This Is Going!
A Score 5 paper uses organizational patterns to clearly communicate a central idea or story line. The order of information draws the reader effortlessly through the text.	√ The paper employs a logical and effective sequence of ideas. √ The paper contains both an attention-grabbing introduction and a satisfying conclusion. √ The pacing is carefully controlled; the writer slows down to provide explanation or elaboration when appropriate, and increases the pace when necessary. √ Transitions make clear connections and cue the reader to specific relationships between ideas. √ The organizational structure is appropriate to the writer's purpose and audience. √ If present, the title sums up the central idea of the paper in a fresh and thoughtful way.
Score 3	**Close—Wait, I Think I Get It**
A Score 3 paper is reasonably strong; it enables readers to move forward without too much confusion.	√ The paper has an introduction and a conclusion. However, the introduction may not be engaging, and the conclusion may not knit together all the paper's ideas. √ The sequence is logical but predictable and therefore not very compelling. √ The sequence may not consistently support the paper's ideas; readers may reorder sections mentally or provide transitions as they read. √ Pacing is reasonably well done, although the writer may move ahead too quickly or linger over unimportant ideas. √ Transitions between ideas may be unclear. √ If present, the title may be dull or lacking insight.
Score 1	**Hmm. I'm a Little Lost**
A Score 1 paper fails to exhibit a sense of purpose or writing strategy; ideas, details, or events seem to be cobbled together without any internal structure or flow.	√ The sequence is broken; one idea or event does not logically follow another; lack of organizational structure, such as clear paragraph breaks, makes it difficult for readers to understand the progression of ideas or events. √ The paper lacks both a clear introduction to guide readers and a conclusion that sums up ideas at the end. √ Pacing is halting or inconsistent; the writer appears not to know when to slow down or speed up the pace. √ Transitions between ideas are confusing or absent. √ If present, the title does not accurately reflect the content of the paper.

Copyright © 2007 by Holt, Rinehart and Winston. All rights reserved.

SIX TRAITS RUBRIC: 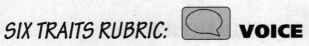 VOICE

Score 5	Yes! I Can Really Hear You
The writing in a Score 5 paper is engaging and conveys the writer's awareness of audience and purpose.	√ The tone of the writing is appropriate for the purpose and audience of the paper. √ The reader is aware of and feels connected to a real person behind the text; if appropriate, the writer takes risks in revealing a personal dimension throughout the piece. √ If the paper is expository or persuasive, the writer shows a strong connection to the topic and explains why readers should care about the issue. √ If the paper is narrative, the point of view is sincere, interesting, and compelling.
Score 3	**Close. Try Again With Feeling**
The writing in a Score 3 paper is reasonably genuine but does not reveal any excitement or connection with the issue; the resulting paper is pleasant but not truly engaging.	√ The writer offers generalities instead of personal insights; as a result, the writing feels impersonal. √ The writer uses neutral language and a flat tone. √ The writer communicates in an earnest and pleasing manner, yet takes no risks; the reader does not feel inspired or engaged. √ Expository or persuasive writing does not reveal the writer's engagement with the topic; there is no attempt to build credibility with the audience. √ Narrative writing fails to reveal a fresh or individual perspective.
Score 1	**Hmm. I Can Barely Hear You**
The writing in a Score 1 paper is mechanical or wooden. The writer appears indifferent to the topic and the audience.	√ The writer shows no concern with the audience; the voice may be inappropriate for the intended reader. √ The development of the topic is so limited that no identifiable point of view is present, or the writing is so short that it offers little but a general introduction of the topic. √ The writer seems to speak in a monotone, using a voice that suppresses all excitement about the message or topic. √ Although the writing may communicate on a functional level, it is ordinary and takes no risks. √ Expository or persuasive writing may lack accurate information or use overly technical language. Narrative writing may lack a point of view and fail to inspire interest.

Copyright © 2007 by Holt, Rinehart and Winston. All rights reserved.

SIX TRAITS RUBRIC: **WORD CHOICE**

Score 5	**Yes! Your Words Come Through Loud and Clear**
In a Score 5 paper, words are precise, engaging, and unaffected. They convey the writer's message in an interesting and effective way.	√ All words are specific and appropriate. In all instances, the writer has taken care to choose the right words or phrases. √ The paper's language is natural, not overdone; it never shows a lack of control. Clichés and jargon are rarely used. √ The paper contains energetic verbs; precise nouns and modifiers provide clarity. √ The writer uses vivid words and phrases, including sensory details; such language creates distinct images in the reader's mind.
Score 3	**Close—With a Little Polish Your Words Will Shine**
Despite its lack of flair, the writing in a Score 3 paper gets the message across because it is functional and clear.	√ Words are correct and generally adequate but lack originality or precision. √ Familiar words and phrases do not grab the reader's interest or imagination. Occasional use of lively verbs and phrases perks things up, but the language does not consistently sparkle. √ Attempts at engaging or academic language may seem overly showy or pretentious. √ The writing contains passive verbs and basic nouns and adjectives, and it lacks precise adverbs.
Score 1	**Hmm. I Don't Understand What You Mean**
The limited vocabulary in a Score 1 paper prevents readers from understanding the writer's message. The writer's struggle for words keeps readers from making connections.	√ Vague language communicates an imprecise or incomplete message or understanding of the topic. The reader feels confused and unsure of the writer's purpose. √ Words are used incorrectly. In addition, frequent misuse of parts of speech limits readers' comprehension. √ Excessive repetition or redundancy distracts readers from the message. √ The writing overuses jargon or clichés.

Copyright © 2007 by Holt, Rinehart and Winston. All rights reserved.

SIX TRAITS RUBRIC: SENTENCE FLUENCY

Score 5	Yes! The Sentences Really Flow
Sentences in a Score 5 paper are thoughtfully constructed, and sentence structure is varied throughout. When read aloud, the writing is fluent and rhythmic.	√ The writer constructs sentences so that meaning is clear to the reader. √ Sentences vary in length and in structure. √ Varied sentence beginnings add interest and clarity. √ The writing has a steady rhythm; the reader is able to read the text effortlessly without confusion or stumbling. √ Dialogue, if used, is natural. Any fragments are used purposefully and contribute to the paper's style. √ Thoughtful connectives and transitions between sentences reveal how the papers' ideas work together.
Score 3	**Close—I'm Feel Like I'm Drifting Off Course**
The text of a Score 3 paper maintains a steady rhythm but the reader may find it flat or mechanical rather than fluent or musical.	√ Sentences are usually grammatical and unified, but they are routine rather than artful. The writer has not paid a great deal of attention to how the sentences sound. √ There is some variation in sentence length and structure as well as in sentence beginnings. Not all sentences are constructed exactly the same way. √ The reader may have to search for transitional words and phrases that show how sentences relate to one another. Sometimes, such context clues are entirely absent when they should be present. √ Although sections of the paper invite expressive oral reading, the reader may also encounter many stilted or awkward sections.
Score 1	**Hmm. I'm a Little Lost**
The reader of a Score 1 paper will encounter challenges in reading the choppy or confusing text; meaning may be significantly obscured by the errors in sentence construction.	√ The sentences do not "hang together." They are run-on, incomplete, monotonous, or awkward. √ Phrasing often sounds too singsong, not natural. The paper does not allow for expressive oral reading. √ Nearly all the sentences begin the same way, and they may all follow the same pattern (e.g. subject-verb-object). The end result may be a monotonous repetition of sounds. √ Endless connectives or a complete lack of connectives creates a confused muddle of language.

Copyright © 2007 by Holt, Rinehart and Winston. All rights reserved.

SIX TRAITS RUBRIC: CONVENTIONS

Score 5	It's Nearly Perfect!
Standard writing conventions in a Score 5 paper are used correctly and in a way that aids the reader's understanding. Any errors tend to be minor; the piece is nearly ready for publication.	√ Paragraphing is regular and enhances the organization of the paper. √ Grammar and usage are correct and add clarity to the text as a whole. Sometimes the writer may manipulate conventions in a controlled way—especially grammar and spelling—for stylistic effect. √ Punctuation is accurate; it enables the reader to move though the text with understanding and ease. √ The writer's understanding of capitalization rules is evident throughout the paper. √ Most words, even difficult ones, are spelled correctly. √ The writing is long and complex enough to show the writer using a wide range of convention skills successfully.
Score 3	**Close—I Found a Few Errors**
The writer of a Score 3 paper exhibits an awareness of a limited set of standard writing conventions and uses them to enhance the papers' readability. Some errors distract and confuse readers. Moderate editing is required before publication.	√ Paragraphs are used but may begin in the wrong places, or sections that should be separate paragraphs are run together. √ Conventions may not always be correct; however, problems with grammar and usage are usually not serious enough to distort meaning. √ End marks are usually correct, but other punctuation marks, such as commas, apostrophes, semi-colons, and parentheses, may be missing or wrong. √ Common words are usually spelled correctly. √ Most words are capitalized correctly, but the writer's command of capitalization skills is inconsistent.
Score 1	**Hmm. I'm Distracted By Too Many Errors**
In a Score 1 paper there are errors in spelling, punctuation, grammar and usage, and paragraphing that seriously impede the reader's comprehension. Extensive editing is required for publication.	√ Paragraphing is missing, uneven, or too frequent. Most of the paragraphs do not reinforce or support the organizational structure of the paper. √ Errors in grammar and usage are very common and distracting; such errors also affect the paper's meaning. √ Punctuation, including terminal punctuation, is often missing or incorrect. √ Even common words are frequently misspelled. √ Capitalization is haphazard or reveals the writer's understanding of only the simplest rules. √ The paper must be read once just to decode the language and then again to capture the paper's meaning.

Copyright © 2007 by Holt, Rinehart and Winston. All rights reserved.

STUDENT/SELF-EVALUATION

Student/Self-Evaluation Rubrics for the Six Traits

Use these rubrics to evaluate your own writing. If you have a strong paper, you will be able to answer "yes" to the questions in the first box. Be honest! If your answers are "no," then go on to the next box. The questions in the second and third boxes will help you identify where your paper needs more work.

SIX TRAITS RUBRIC: IDEAS AND CONTENT

5 It's Crystal Clear!

√ Is my topic clearly focused—neither too broad nor too narrow—for a paper of its kind?

√ Are my ideas are original, interesting, and creative?

√ Do I draw from personal experience or knowledge.

√ Are my details are insightful and well chosen? Or are they obvious, predictable, or clichéd—not good?

√ Is my development of the topic thorough and logical? Have I anticipated and answered the reader's questions?

√ Are my supporting details accurate and relevant? Does my every detail contribute to the whole?

3 Close—It's Getting There

√ Could I develop my topic a little better? Do I make my readers work to figure out my purpose and predict how ideas will develop?

√ Are my supporting details present but maybe too vague? Could they really illustrate the main idea or theme better?

√ Do I refer to my own experience or knowledge but maybe fail to push beyond the obvious to more specific ideas?

√ Are my ideas understandable but maybe not detailed, elaborated upon, or personalized? Do I need to work on understanding my topic or task more?

√ Do I stray from the topic? Are my ideas too general? Do I force readers to rely on what they already know to make sense of the paper?

1 Hmm. What Am I Trying to Say?

√ Have I forgotten to decide on a topic or main idea? Does my paper read like rough draft or brainstorming notes?

√ Is my thesis a vague statement about the topic or a restatement of a prompt? Does it need more support, detail, or insight?

√ Do I need to add information? Do I make my readers work too hard to make connections?

√ Is my text rambling and repetitious? Are my ideas not developed enough? Is the paper too short?

√ Does every idea and detail in my paper seem equally weighted? Do my ideas add up to a main idea, thesis, or theme?

Copyright © 2007 by Holt, Rinehart and Winston. All rights reserved.

STUDENT/SELF-EVALUATION

SIX TRAITS RUBRIC: ORGANIZATION

5 Yes! I Can See Where This Is Going!

√ Does my paper use a logical and effective sequence of ideas?

√ Does the paper contain both an attention-grabbing introduction and a satisfying conclusion?

√ Is my pacing carefully controlled? Do I slow down to provide explanation or elaboration when appropriate, and increase the pace when necessary?

√ Do my transitions make clear connections and cue the reader to specific relationships between ideas?

√ Is my organizational structure appropriate to my purpose and audience?

√ If present, does my title sum up the central idea of the paper in a fresh way?

3 Close—Wait, I Think I Get It

√ Does my paper have both an introduction and a conclusion? Are they as engaging and coherent as they can be?

√ Is my sequence logical but predictable? Could it be more compelling?

√ Does my sequence fail to consistently support my pa\per's ideas? Do I make my readers reorder sections mentally or provide transitions as they read?

√ Is my pacing reasonably well done? Do I move ahead too quickly or linger over unimportant ideas?

√ Are the transitions between ideas clear enough.

√ If present, is my title maybe a little dull or lacking insight?

1 Hmm. I'm a Little Lost

√ Is the sequence in my paper is broken— maybe one idea or event does not logically follow another? Does it lack organizational structure, such as clear paragraph breaks?

√ Does my paper lacks a clear introduction to guide readers and a conclusion that sums up ideas at the end?

√ Is my pacing halting or inconsistent? Do I know when to slow down or speed up the pace—in order to help my readers understand?

√ Are the transitions between my ideas confusing or absent?

√ If present, does my title accurately reflect the content of the paper? If not, why?

Copyright © 2007 by Holt, Rinehart and Winston. All rights reserved.

STUDENT/SELF-EVALUATION

SIX TRAITS RUBRIC: 🗨 VOICE

---

5 Yes! I Can Really Hear My Own Voice

√ Is my tone of the writing appropriate for the purpose and audience of the paper?

√ Do I reveal myself as a real person behind the text? Do I take risks in revealing my personality throughout the piece?

√ If my paper is expository or persuasive, do I show a strong connection to the topic and explain why readers should care about the issue?

√ If my paper is narrative, is my point of view sincere, interesting, and compelling?

3 Close. I Need to Try Again With Feeling

√ Do I offer only generalities instead of personal insights? Does my writing feel impersonal?

√ Do I use neutral language and a flat tone instead of an interested lively one?

√ Do I communicate in an earnest and pleasing manner, but forget to risks? Do I need to inspire or engage my reader more?

√ Do I really share my own interest with the topic? Do I need to build more credibility with the audience?

√ Does my narrative fail to reveal a fresh or individual perspective?

1 Hmm. I Can Barely Hear Myself Speaking

√ Is it true that I don't really think about the audience—that I use a voice that may not be appropriate for the intended reader?

√ Is the development of my topic too limited, so that no clear point of view is present? Is my writing is so short that readers don't get to know me?

√ Do I seem to speak in a monotone, using a voice that lacks excitement about the message or topic?

√ Does my expository or persuasive writing lack accurate information or use overly technical language? Is my narrative writing lacking a point of view and failing to inspire interest?

Copyright © 2007 by Holt, Rinehart and Winston. All rights reserved.

SIX TRAITS RUBRIC: WORD CHOICE

5 Yes! My Words Come Through Loud and Clear

√ Are all my words specific and appropriate? In all instances, have I taken care to choose the right words or phrases?

√ Is my paper's language controlled and natural, not overdone? Do I rarely use clichés and jargon?

√ Does my paper contain energetic verbs, precise nouns, and clear modifiers?

√ Do I use vivid words and phrases, including sensory details to create distinct images in the reader's mind?

3 Close—With a Little Polish My Words Will Shine

√ Are my words correct and generally adequate but maybe lacking in originality or precision?

√ Do I use familiar words and phrases that do not grab the reader's interest or imagination or only occasionally use of lively verbs and phrases to perks things?

√ Do my attempts at using engaging or academic language seem overly showy?

√ Does my writing contain passive verbs and basic nouns and adjectives? Does it lack precise adverbs.

1 Hmm. Even I Don't Understand What I Mean

√ Is my language perhaps too vague instead of precise? Does my vague language make the reader feel confused and unsure of my purpose?

√ Are some of my words or parts of speech used incorrectly?

√ Do I repeat myself or use certain words too much?

√ Have I used unexplained jargon or clichés.

Copyright © 2007 by Holt, Rinehart and Winston. All rights reserved.

SIX TRAITS RUBRIC: SENTENCE FLUENCY

5 Yes! My Sentences Really Flow

√ Have I constructed sentences so that meaning is clear to the reader?

√ Do my sentences vary in length and in structure?

√ Do I use varied sentence beginnings to add interest and clarity?

√ Does my writing have a steady rhythm? Is my reader able to read the text effortlessly without confusion or stumbling?

√ Is my use of dialogue natural? Do I use sentence fragments thoughtfully?

√ Do I use clear connectives and transitions between sentences to reveal how the papers' ideas work together?

3 Close—I'm Feel Like I'm Drifting Off Course

√ Are my sentences usually grammatical and unified but dull? Have I forgotten to pay enough attention to how the sentences sound?

√ Is there some variation in sentence length and structure as well as in sentence beginnings? Or are all my sentences constructed exactly the same way?

√ Do I make my reader search for transitional words and phrases that show how sentences relate to one another? Do I forget to use context clues?

√ Even though I have written expressively, are there passages with stilted or awkward sentences?

1 Hmm. I'm a Little Lost

√ Do my sentences just not "hang together"? Have I used run-on, incomplete, monotonous, or awkward sentences?

√ Does my phrasing often sound too singsong? Is my paper kind of dull to read aloud?

√ Do most of the sentences begin the same way and follow the same pattern (e.g. subject-verb-object)?

√ Have I used too many connectives or too few—so that my writing sometimes sounds confused?

Copyright © 2007 by Holt, Rinehart and Winston. All rights reserved.

SIX TRAITS RUBRIC: CONVENTIONS

5 Yes! It's Nearly Perfect!

√ Is my paragraphing regular? Does it enhance the organization of the paper?

√ Are my grammar and usage correct? Do they add clarity and style to the text?

√ Is my punctuation accurate and does it enables the reader to move though the text with understanding and ease?

√ Is my understanding of capitalization rules evident throughout the paper?

√ Are most words, even difficult ones, are spelled correctly?

√ Is my writing long and complex enough to show that I understand a wide range of convention skills?

3 Close—I Found a Few Errors

√ Do I run together ideas that should be in separate paragraphs? Do I start paragraphs in the middle of an idea?

√ Does my writing have a few grammar and usage errors—but not enough to confuse my readers?

√ Are my end marks usually in the correct place, but maybe other punctuation marks (such as commas, apostrophes, semi-colons, and parentheses) are missing or wrong?

√ Have I spelled common words correctly for the most part?

√ Are most words are capitalized correctly, but my command of capitalization skills is a little shaky?

1 Hmm. I'm Distracted By Too Many Errors

√ Am I missing formal paragraphs? Do my paragraphs "forget" to support my content or organization?

√ Have I made a lot of errors in grammar and usage? Are there enough errors to distract or confuse the reader?

√ Is my punctuation, including end marks often missing or incorrect?

√ Have I misspelled common words?

√ Have I consistently made errors in capitalization?

√ Does my paper need to be read once just to decode the language and then again to understand my meaning?

Copyright © 2007 by Holt, Rinehart and Winston. All rights reserved.

STUDENT/SELF-EVALUATION

SIX TRAITS RUBRIC:
PRESENTATION/PUBLICATION

5 Yes! My Paper Is Clear and Pleasing to the Eye

√ If my paper is handwritten, is the slant of my writing consistent and my spacing between words uniform?

√ If my paper is word-processed, have I used an appropriate font and font size?

√ Have I used enough white space (spacing, margins) so that my paper is easy to read?

√ If I have included a title, headings or subheadings, bullets and page numbering, are they consistent and do they make the paper easy to read?

√ If I have used graphs, tables, maps, or other graphics in my writing, are they clear and placed logically in my paper?

3 Close—My Paper is a Little Cluttered

√ Is my handwriting readable but maybe a little sloppy or inconsistent?

√ Have I used too many fonts or a font size that is hard to read?

√ Have I got too much or too little white space—my margins are too wide or too small? Have I got too much or too little space between paragraphs?

√ Even though I use titles, headings or subheadings, bullets and page numbering, are they inconsistently used or maybe they get in the way of the reading?

√ Have I placed graphs, tables, maps, or other graphics in the wrong places or too far from the text they help explain? Do they take up too much space or are they too small to read?

1 Hmm. I'm Distracted By the Way the Page Looks

√ Has poor handwriting made my paper too difficult to read?

√ Has my use of interesting or too many fonts and font sizes made my paper difficult to read?

√ Is my spacing too random or confusing for readers to see and read the text?

√ Does my paper need a title, headings or subheadings, bullets, or page numbers that would help readers get through the paper?

√ Do my visuals (graphs, tables, maps, or other graphics) mislead or confuse my readers? Are they appropriate or too technical? Should I leave them out or find new ones?

Copyright © 2007 by Holt, Rinehart and Winston. All rights reserved.

SIX TRAITS RUBRIC FLASHCARDS

Encourage students to use these flashcards to familiarize themselves with the six traits and with the level five rubric for each trait. Students may use the flashcards as study guides, or they may use them during the revision stage of the writing process. Encourage students to work in pairs or teams to quiz each other about the six traits and the criteria for a level five paper.

For each of the flashcards, you will find the front of the flashcard on the right-hand page and the back on the following left-hand page.

IDEAS AND CONTENT

Definition:

Ideas and content are the building blocks of a good paper. The ideas are the thoughts and connections a writer wants the audience to understand. The content is the way the ideas are expressed and presented.

Related terms: *main idea, details, purpose, audience*

ORGANIZATION

Definition:

Organization is the way in which writers structure their ideas and content. It is like a frame or outline. It guides readers through the content and highlights the ideas.

Related terms: *chronological order, logical order, special order, order of importance*

Copyright © 2007 by Holt, Rinehart and Winston. All rights reserved.

SIX TRAITS RUBRIC FLASHCARDS

Score 5	Six Traits Rubric: Ideas and Content
A paper that has clear ideas and content is clear, focused, and interesting. It presents relevant and concrete details that catch and maintain the reader's interest and support a clear main idea, theme, or story line.	√ The topic is clearly focused—neither too broad nor too narrow—for a paper of its kind. √ The ideas are original, interesting, and creative. √ The writer draws from personal experience or knowledge. √ Key details are insightful and well chosen; they are not obvious, predictable, or clichéd. √ The development of the topic is thorough and logical; the writer anticipates and answers the reader's questions. √ Supporting details are accurate and relevant; every detail contributes to the whole.

Score 5	Six Traits Rubric: Organization
A Score 5 paper uses organizational patterns to clearly communicate a central idea or story line. The order of information draws the reader effortlessly through the text.	√ The paper employs a logical and effective sequence of ideas. √ The paper contains both an attention-grabbing introduction and a satisfying conclusion. √ The pacing is carefully controlled; the writer slows down to provide explanation or elaboration when appropriate, and increases the pace when necessary. √ Transitions make clear connections and cue the reader to specific relationships between ideas. √ The organizational structure is appropriate to the writer's purpose and audience. √ If present, the title sums up the central idea of the paper in a fresh and thoughtful way.

Copyright © 2007 by Holt, Rinehart and Winston. All rights reserved.

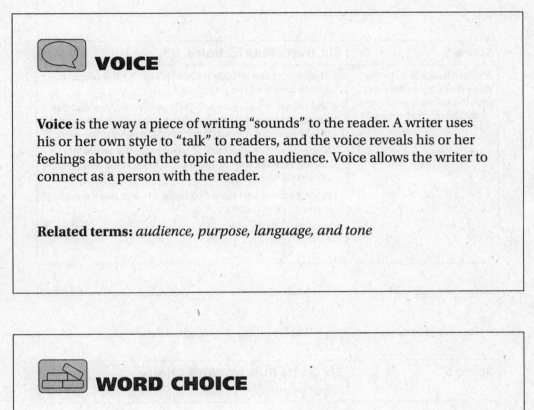

VOICE

Voice is the way a piece of writing "sounds" to the reader. A writer uses his or her own style to "talk" to readers, and the voice reveals his or her feelings about both the topic and the audience. Voice allows the writer to connect as a person with the reader.

Related terms: *audience, purpose, language, and tone*

WORD CHOICE

Word choice is how a writer expresses his or her voice. Words are the building blocks of any piece of writing. The words a writer chooses help create a clear voice and engage the reader. Choosing a precise word is like landing an arrow right in the center of the target.

Related terms: *connotation, denotation, idiom, jargon, loaded language, tired language or clichés*

Copyright © 2007 by Holt, Rinehart and Winston. All rights reserved.

SIX TRAITS RUBRIC FLASHCARDS

Score 5	Six Traits Rubric: Voice
A paper that has a strong voice is engaging and conveys the writer's awareness of audience and purpose.	√ The tone of the writing is appropriate for the purpose and audience of the paper. √ The reader is aware of and feels connected to a real person behind the text; if appropriate, the writer takes risks in revealing a personal dimension throughout the piece. √ If the paper is expository or persuasive, the writer shows a strong connection to the topic and explains why readers should care about the issue. √ If the paper is narrative, the point of view is sincere, interesting, and compelling.

Score 5	Six Traits Rubric: Word Choice
In a paper with strong word choice, the words are precise, engaging, and unaffected. They convey the writer's message in an interesting and effective way	√ All words are specific and appropriate. In all instances, the writer has taken care to choose the right words or phrases. √ The paper's language is natural, not overdone; it never shows a lack of control. Clichés and jargon are rarely used. √ The paper contains energetic verbs; precise nouns and modifiers provide clarity. √ The writer uses vivid words and phrases, including sensory details; such language creates distinct images in the reader's mind.

Copyright © 2007 by Holt, Rinehart and Winston. All rights reserved.

SENTENCE FLUENCY

Sentence fluency is how the sentences in a piece of writing flow together. Sentence fluency adds rhythm and style to writing. Good writers use a mixture of short and long sentences, as well as sentences that start with phrases or clauses, to create a natural rhythm and style that engages readers.

Related terms: *sentence fragments, run-on sentences, stringy sentences, choppy sentences, wordy sentence*

 **CONVENTIONS**

Conventions are the agreed rules of paragraphing, usage, grammar, spelling, and punctuation that good writers follow. Conventions help writers make their meanings clear.

Related terms: *paragraphing, grammar, usage, punctuation, capitalization, spelling*

 PRESENTATION/PUBLISHING

Presentation and publishing are the last things to consider when preparing a paper for readers.

Related terms: *handwritten, word-processed, font, font size, white space, margins, titles, subtitles or subheadings, tables, graphs, graphics*

Copyright © 2007 by Holt, Rinehart and Winston. All rights reserved.

SIX TRAITS RUBRIC FLASHCARDS

Score 5	Six Traits Rubric: Sentence Fluency
Sentences in a well-written paper are thoughtfully constructed, and sentence structure is varied throughout. When read aloud, the writing is fluent and rhythmic.	√ The writer constructs sentences so that meaning is clear to the reader. √ Sentences vary in length and in structure. √ Varied sentence beginnings add interest and clarity. √ The writing has a steady rhythm; the reader is able to read the text effortlessly without confusion or stumbling. √ Dialogue, if used, is natural. Any fragments are used purposefully and contribute to the paper's style. √ Thoughtful connectives and transitions between sentences reveal how the papers' ideas work together.

Score 5	Six Traits Rubric: Conventions
Standard writing conventions in a well-written paper are used correctly and in a way that aids the reader's understanding. Any errors tend to be minor; the piece is nearly ready for publication.	√ Paragraphing is regular and enhances the organization of the paper. √ Grammar and usage are correct and add clarity to the text as a whole. √ Punctuation is accurate; it enables the reader to move though the text with understanding and ease. √ The writer's understanding of capitalization rules is evident throughout the paper. √ Most words, even difficult ones, are spelled correctly. √ The writing is long and complex enough to show the writer's successful use of a wide range of convention skills.

Score 5	Six Traits Rubric: Presentation/Publishing
A paper that is presented and published well has a clean, uncluttered appearance and is easy to read.	√ If the paper is handwritten, the slant of the writing consistent and the spacing between words is uniform. √ If the paper is word-processed, an appropriate font and font size are used. √ The paper contains enough white space (line spacing, margins) so that the text is set off nicely and easy to read. √ Any title, subtitles or subheadings, bullets and page numbering are used consistently so that they make the paper easy to navigate. √ Any graphs, tables, maps, or other graphics are clear and placed logically in the paper.

Copyright © 2007 by Holt, Rinehart and Winston. All rights reserved.

Evaluation Chart

You can fill in the chart below as you evaluate your own or another student's writing.

Directions: In the table below, write the scores you give the paper for its execution of each of the six writing traits. (The highest score is 5; the lowest is 1.)

Scores	
Ideas and Content	
Organization	
Voice	
Word Choice	
Sentence Fluency	
Conventions	

Directions: Below write some comments that explain the scores you wrote above. Use specific examples from the text to support your evaluations.

Comments:

Ideas and Content:_____

_____

_____

Organization: _____

_____

_____

Voice: _____

_____

_____

Word Choice: _____

_____

_____

Sentence Fluency: _____

_____

Conventions: _____

_____

Sum It Up: Overall I thought the paper was_____

_____

_____

Copyright © 2007 by Holt, Rinehart and Winston. All rights reserved.

SIX TRAITS: **WORKSHEETS**

The worksheets that appear in this section are designed to support students in combining the six traits and the writing process.

Copyright © 2007 by Holt, Rinehart and Winston. All rights reserved.

SIX TRAITS: IDEAS AND CONTENT

Type of Writing: Expository, Persuasive, or Narrative

Clustering-Word Web
Directions: Fill in the center circle with a word related to your topic. Then fill in the other circles with related words or ideas. Add more circles, if necessary. Draw lines between the circles to show the connections.

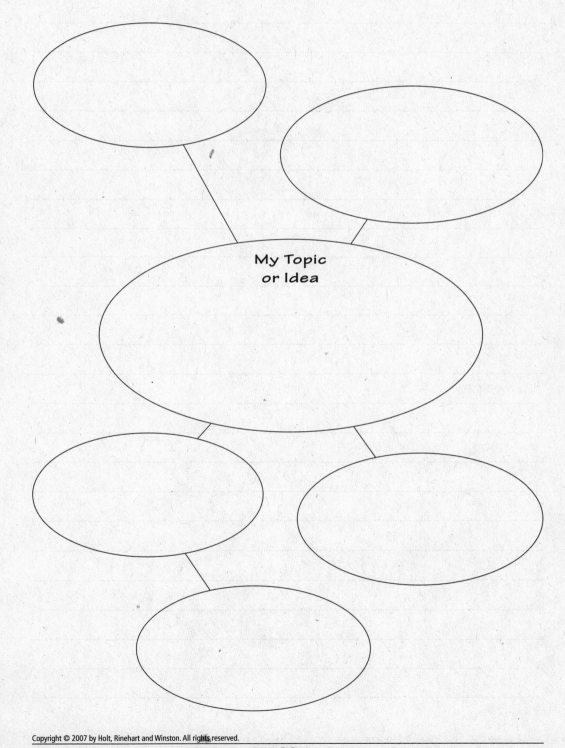

My Topic
or Idea

Copyright © 2007 by Holt, Rinehart and Winston. All rights reserved.

SIX TRAITS:  IDEAS AND CONTENT

Type of Writing: Expository, Persuasive, or Narrative

Brainstorming-Freewriting
Directions: Use the lines below to write about your topic without stopping for about five minutes. Write down every idea that pops into your head. Don't judge yourself! After your time is up, reread your ideas. Use a colored pencil or pen to circle or underline ideas that you want to develop in your paper.

_____

_____

_____

_____

_____

_____

_____

_____

_____

_____

_____

_____

_____

_____

_____

_____

_____

_____

_____

_____

_____

_____

_____

_____

Copyright © 2007 by Holt, Rinehart and Winston. All rights reserved.

SIX TRAITS: 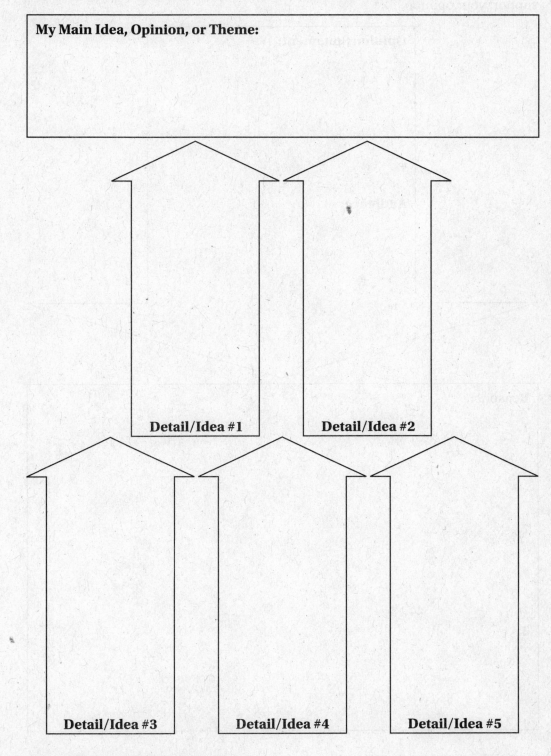 IDEAS AND CONTENT

Type of Writing: Expository, Persuasive, or Narrative

What's Your Point?: Identifying the Main Idea

Directions: Use the graphic organizer below to refine your thoughts into a main idea. Start at the bottom. Fill in the boxes with details and information. In the box labeled "Main Idea," write the idea that the other boxes support.

My Main Idea, Opinion, or Theme:

Detail/Idea #1

Detail/Idea #2

Detail/Idea #3

Detail/Idea #4

Detail/Idea #5

Copyright © 2007 by Holt, Rinehart and Winston. All rights reserved.

Type of Writing: Persuasive

Stating an Opinion

Directions: Use the graphic organizer below to identify an opinion statement and the reasons that support it. In the arrow at the top, write your opinion statement and identify the audience for your paper. In the large box, list all the reasons that support your opinion.

Opinion Statement:

Audience:

Reasons:

1.

2.

3.

Copyright © 2007 by Holt, Rinehart and Winston. All rights reserved.

SIX TRAITS: 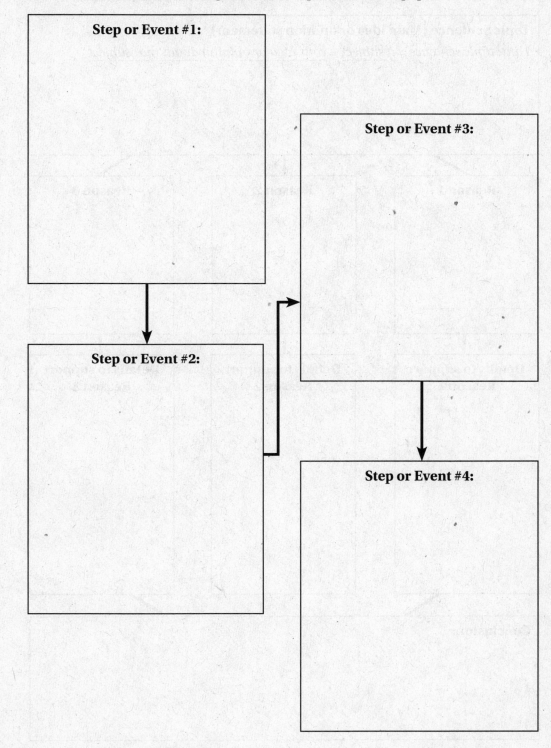 ORGANIZATION

Type of Writing: Expository or Narrative

Finding the Flow: How-to Writing/Flow Chart

Directions: Complete this flow chart by writing the steps or events in chronological order. Include any details that help describe the steps or events. You may add more boxes or continue the organizer on a separate sheet of paper.

Step or Event #1:

Step or Event #2:

Step or Event #3:

Step or Event #4:

Copyright © 2007 by Holt, Rinehart and Winston. All rights reserved.

Type of Writing: Expository or Persuasive

Organizing Your Reasons

Directions: Write your topic sentence (your main idea or opinion statement) in the top box. Write each of your reasons and any supporting details or evidence in the separate boxes below it. Then, write your conclusion in the bottom box.

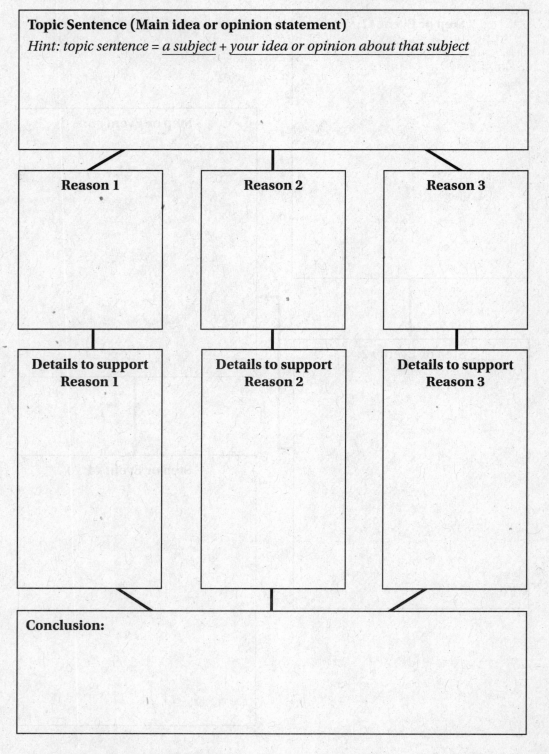

Topic Sentence (Main idea or opinion statement)

Hint: topic sentence = a subject + your idea or opinion about that subject

Reason 1

Reason 2

Reason 3

Details to support Reason 1

Details to support Reason 2

Details to support Reason 3

Conclusion:

Copyright © 2007 by Holt, Rinehart and Winston. All rights reserved.

Type of Writing: Expository or Persuasive

Organizing Reasons by Order of Importance

Directions: Write your second most important reason in the top box. Write your least important reason in the middle box. Write your most important reason in the bottom box. On a separate sheet of paper, try experimenting with a different order, such as least-to-most important reason. Which order works best?

Hint: Most people remember best what they have read last.

My main idea or opinion statement:

_____

_____

My most important reason:

My second-most-important reason:

My least important reason:

Copyright © 2007 by Holt, Rinehart and Winston. All rights reserved.

SIX TRAITS:  ORGANIZATION

Type of Writing: Expository or Persuasive

Using an Outline

Directions: Write each reason in the outline below. Under each reason, write in the supporting details or information. Try to elaborate on each item of support. For example, how does the supporting information prove your point?

Main Idea or Opinion Statement:

_____

_____

_____

Reason #1: _____

   Supporting Detail #1 _____

   Elaboration: _____

   Supporting Detail #2 _____

   Elaboration: _____

Reason #2: _____

   Supporting Detail #1 _____

   Supporting Detail #2 _____

Reason #3: _____

   Supporting Detail #1 _____

   Elaboration: _____

   Supporting Detail #2 _____

   Elaboration: _____

Summing It Up:

Copyright © 2007 by Holt, Rinehart and Winston. All rights reserved.

SIX TRAITS: 💬 VOICE

Type of Writing: Expository, Persuasive, or Narrative

Identifying Tone

Directions: Read the three passages below. Then choose one or more of the words from the box at the bottom of the page to identify its tone. (Or choose tone words of your own.) Write the word or words on the line, along with a statement that explains why you selected the tone.

Passage 1: Requiring students to volunteer or to complete community service in order to graduate is really unfair. While I understand how important it is to give back to the community, I would like to point out that many students already do that—and without getting one bit of credit. Many of my friends help the community through scouting and church groups. They plant trees, clean up playgrounds, and take meals to seniors. To expect them to take on additional community service is just plain unfair.

I would describe the tone as _____ because_____.

Passage 2: Of course everyone loves animals! Duh! Some people like dogs, some like cats, and some like rats. Whatever. You probably own a couple of animals yourself. And why not? After all, scientists and researchers have discovered that pets help lower people's blood pressure and reduce their anxieties. They say that pets are as good as a yoga class. Me? I've got three dogs and no worries—except of course, where's the leash?

I would describe the tone as _____ because_____.

Passage 3: An ink-cartridge recycling program can help improve our environment. By reusing those little plastic cases, we can keep them out of our landfills. By keeping them out of the dump, we also keep toxic chemicals in the ink from leaking into the ground and into our water supplies. Some ink-cartridge makers are dragging their feet, however, and it is up to consumers to light a fire under them and get them to take responsibility for their products.

I would describe the tone as _____ because_____.

reasonable	whiny	respectful	friendly	formal
informal	cheeky	conversational	thoughtful	mean

 Try your skills of creating a voice. Choose one of the passages above and rewrite in a different voice. Rewrite your passage on a separate sheet of paper.

Copyright © 2007 by Holt, Rinehart and Winston. All rights reserved.

Type of Writing: Expository, Persuasive, or Narrative

Recognizing Connotations

Directions: Use a dictionary and the sample sentences below to determine the connotations of the words in the first column in the organizer below. The first row of the chart gives you an example.

Word	Definition	Sample Sentence	Connotation (Revised Definition)
dawdle	*to waste time*	After school the children dawdled on the playground.	*When you dawdle, you waste time in a pleasant and harmless way.*
1. naughty		The naughty puppy barked and then fell off the cushion it was chewing on.	
2. challenging		Lauren found the extra-credit section on the test to be particularly challenging.	
3. oozed		For weeks after the flood, the ground oozed under our feet.	
4. recognition		At his retirement, the teacher received the recognition he deserved.	
5. sensitive		Margot is so sensitive that she gets her feelings hurt all the time.	

Use the words in the chart above in sentences of your own. Write your sentences on a separate sheet of paper. Then explain how did the words' connotations affected the way you used them.

Copyright © 2007 by Holt, Rinehart and Winston. All rights reserved.

Type of Writing: Expository, Persuasive, or Narrative

Avoiding Loaded Language, Jargon, and Clichés

Directions: Read each sentence below. Underline the loaded language, jargon, or cliché (or tired word) that appears in each sentence. On the line provided, write LL for loaded language, J for jargon, or C for cliché. (See p. 11 for help with these terms.)

_____ **1.** Mr. Johnson really let the cat out of the bag when he told Linda about the surprise party.

_____ **2.** How can honest, hard-working Americans compete in a global economy?

_____ **3.** Dennis will run the numbers again to find the error.

_____ **4.** Bonnie looked as pretty as a picture for her graduation photo.

_____ **5.** After our trip to the beach, my face was as red as a lobster.

_____ **6.** Wall Street had a good day today—both the Dow and NASDAQ were up.

_____ **7.** After you log on, enter your password and your PIN.

_____ **8.** Hospitals are full of quacks who don't know their stethoscopes from their elbows.

_____ **9.** Nina was as mad as a wet hen when she realized she missed the application date.

_____ **10.** An encounter with an incompetent bureaucrat can waste your whole day.

_____ **11.** Scan the bar code and see what price comes up.

_____ **12.** That can was as flat as a pancake after the bus ran over it.

_____ **13.** Your dress is great! It's very unique!

_____ **14.** Those fat cat politicians are trying to raise our taxes again.

_____ **15.** You can't possibly expect to get good food at a restaurant that cater to wannabes and posers like this one does.

ON YOUR OWN! Choose ten sentences from the exercise above and rewrite them without the loaded language, jargon, or cliché. Write your sentences on a separate sheet of paper and review them with a friend.

Copyright © 2007 by Holt, Rinehart and Winston. All rights reserved.

SIX TRAITS: SENTENCE FLUENCY

Type of Writing: Expository, Persuasive, or Narrative

Avoiding Passive Voice

Directions: On the short line provided, identify the voice in each sentence as AV for active voice or PV for passive voice. If a sentence is PV, rewrite it in active voice on the line.

_____ **1.** The tennis ball was served by Sharmaine.

_____

_____ **2.** Dad cooked lasagne for the family last night.

_____

_____ **3.** The class was attended by several new people.

_____

_____ **4.** The art in the museum is viewed by many tourists.

_____

_____ **5.** Our pecan tree was pruned by a tree trimmer.

_____

_____ **6.** The dog was given its rabies vaccination by the veterinarian.

_____

_____ **7.** The computer was fixed by the technician.

_____

_____ **8.** Glenna gave a lecture on her visit to the Southwest.

_____

_____ **9.** Her parents praised her for her good attitude.

_____

Directions: Passive voice is often indicated by the use of "to be" verbs. Read the passage below and underline all the "to be" verbs. Then decide if the verbs are helping verbs that create a passive voice. On a separate sheet of paper, rewrite the paragraph, making all the sentences in active voice.

[1] The arctic tundra is characterized by long winters, little snow, and low temperatures. [2] Warm summer temperatures thaw the tundra's surface soil but not the subsoil, or permafrost. [3] Therefore, drainage is hindered by flat and partially frozen ground. [4] Ponds and bogs are formed by standing water. [5] Typical artic vegetation includes low plants, such as cotton grass, sedge, and lichens. [6] Soil disturbances such as "flowing soil" are caused by thaws and movement of soil. [7] Irregular landforms, such as hummocks, frost boils, and earth stripes, are produced by poorly drained areas. [8] On the soft surface, deep gullies are caused by vehicle tracks. [9] Most arctic vegetation can survive these soil disturbances. [10] Likewise, arctic wildlife is also not deeply affected by these changes.

Copyright © 2007 by Holt, Rinehart and Winston. All rights reserved.

SIX TRAITS: SENTENCE FLUENCY

Type of Writing: Expository, Persuasive, or Narrative

Revising for Sentence Variety

Directions: The sentences in the paragraphs below all have the same construction and roughly the same length. They sound rather dull. On a separate sheet of paper, rewrite and revise the paragraphs by combining sentences to vary the lengths and by beginning some sentences with phrases and clauses. There is no one correct way to revise the paragraphs.

The Populist movement was an American movement. It developed in the 1800s. It began during the depression of the late 1870s. Farmers were losing money then. They formed organized groups. The groups were called Farmers' Alliances. Members of the alliances worked together. They built barns. The barns stored the crops. The crops stayed in the barns until the prices were better. Some alliances included African American farmers. African American farmers could not vote. The alliances welcomed them anyway.

The alliances became powerful at the end of the century. They formed a national political party. They joined forces with another group. It was called the Knights of Labor. The two groups formed the People's Party. Its members were known as Populists. Populists wanted the national government to change. They wanted it to print more paper money. More paper money might raise farm prices. The Populists also wanted a national income tax. Americans did not pay income tax then. It was not a popular idea. Income tax became a reality though. Congress passed an amendment in 1913. It was the sixteenth amendment. It made a national income tax legal. Americans have paid income tax ever since.

Copyright © 2007 by Holt, Rinehart and Winston. All rights reserved.

SIX TRAITS: SENTENCE FLUENCY

Type of Writing: Expository, Persuasive, or Narrative

Revising Run-on Sentences

Directions: Correct the run-on sentences in the following paragraphs by inserting periods and capital letters where needed. Cross out each incorrect comma or lowercase letter, and write the correct period or capital letter above it. Make sure you don't create any sentence fragments! (See p. 14 for help.)

Example: *Our local weatherman is very knowledgeable, he has a degree in meteorology.*

Today when modern meteorologists forecast the weather, they can count on the help of an impressive battery of scientific devices. Weather satellites, for example, relay photographs of cloud formations from all over the world these pictures show where storms are beginning over oceans and deserts the paths of typhoons and hurricanes are tracked the same way. Weather information from all sources is fed into powerful computers, thus the weather can be evaluated with amazing speed.

Our ancestors had no complicated weather instruments they had to rely on their eyes and ears and a few old proverbs and maxims. Their methods were hardly scientific today, for example, no one still believes the old superstition about the groundhog, but we celebrate Groundhog Day just the same. The story goes that if the groundhog sees its shadow on the second day of February, there will be six more months of winter, watch for yourself and see! The behavior of insects, on the other hand, is still a good indicator of temperature because they are cold blooded. Grasshoppers cannot fly when the temperature drops below 55 degrees Fahrenheit if you hear a cricket chirping, count the number of chirps in fourteen seconds and add forty, then you will have the temperature in degrees Fahrenheit.

Today weather forecasting is much more accurate if less charming than it was in the old days, however, the forecasters are still not always right, perhaps because there are so many factors to consider.

Copyright © 2007 by Holt, Rinehart and Winston. All rights reserved.

SIX TRAITS: **SENTENCE FLUENCY**

Type of Writing: Expository, Persuasive, or Narrative

Revising Stringy and Wordy Sentences

Directions: The sentences in the paragraph below are stringy. On a separate sheet of paper, rewrite and revise the stringy sentences by breaking them into two or more sentences or by turning some of the independent clauses into phrases or subordinate clauses. You may add, change, or delete words.

Argentina is a country in South America and it borders the south Atlantic and its capital is Buenos Aires. My friend Leela has been to Argentina, but she went with her family, and her father studied at a university there, but Leela had a great time meeting people, and she got to speak in Spanish. Leela spent time in the city but she also got to go to the countryside and she learned about the life of the cowboys of South America and she was very impressed. Leela wrote a story about her experiences and it is about a character named Tanmoor, and he is an interesting character, but he is from a small town in Argentina, but he wants to move to the big city. The story has an interesting beginning and it opens with Tanmoor's father working on a ranch but he is a vaquero—a cowboy, and the bank wants to put him out of business, and Tanmoor is trying to help save the ranch. Leela clearly did lots of research and she asked a lot of questions and it shows and the story is excellent!

Directions: The sentences in the paragraph below are wordy. On a separate sheet of paper, rewrite and revise the wordy sentences by replacing a group of words with a word, a clause with a phrase, or taking out unnecessary words.

When the daughters of pioneers were young girls, they learned how to sew and cook. Young girls had to learn household skills due to the fact that if they didn't do the chores, the chores wouldn't get done. So girls would attend their mother's instructions with great carefulness and thoughtfulness. They had to do all sorts of chores of the kind that we don't even do anymore like make butter, bake bread, and wash clothes by hand. Today we have machines, which are convenient and easy to use, to do chores that are related to the household. Also in addition, we never have to cook because we can go to the grocery store and buy any kind of food we want, which is already cooked and ready-to-eat. What I mean to say is that life was hard for pioneer women, and we should be grateful that we can just flip a switch, which is so easy, get so many jobs done right away immediately.

Copyright © 2007 by Holt, Rinehart and Winston. All rights reserved.

SIX TRAITS: SENTENCE FLUENCY

Type of Writing: Expository, Persuasive, or Narrative

Choppy Sentences and Sentence Combining

Directions: On the lines provided combine the choppy sentences into one complete sentence by inserting words, prepositional phrases, or conjunctions.

Example: Mount Everest is famous. It is the most famous mountain in the world.

Mount Everest is the most famous mountain in the world.

1. The Himalayas are mountains in Asia. They are the tallest mountains in Asia.

_____

2. Tea bushes grow on slopes. The slopes are of the hills near Darjeeling. The slopes are steep. The hills are fertile.

_____

3. The danger in climbing is great. It comes from the altitude and the cold. The altitude is high. The cold is bitter.

_____

4. Marissa will hike in Rocky Mountain National Park. Mara will hike, too. They will pitch tents. The tents will be pitched in Hidden Valley.

_____

5. Marissa has her own camping equipment. Mara has camping equipment, too. They both know how to use the equipment.

_____

6. The two young women love camping. They also love hiking.

_____

7. Alexander the Great's father was the king. He was the king of Macedonia.

_____

8. Alexander wanted a horse. It was afraid of its own shadow. Alexander wanted to tame it.

_____

9. Alexander turned the horse around. Now it faced the sun. Now it could not see its own shadow. It calmed down.

_____

10. This story is an example. It is the story of Alexander the Great. It tells how he tamed the wild horse. He did it with kindness and compassion.

_____

_____

Copyright © 2007 by Holt, Rinehart and Winston. All rights reserved.

SIX TRAITS: SENTENCE FLUENCY

Type of Writing: Expository, Persuasive, or Narrative

Using Transitional Words and Phrases
To show readers how ideas are connected, writers use transitional words and phrases.

Chronological Order	after, at last, at once, before, eventually, finally, first, later, meanwhile, next, soon, then, when, while
Cause-and-Effect	as a result, because, consequently, for, for this reason, since, so, so that, therefore
Spatial Order	above, across, among, around, before, behind, below, beneath, by, down, here, in, inside, into, near, next to, over, there, under, up
Order of Importance	first, last, mainly, more important, then, to begin with
Comparison	also, and, another, just as, like, likewise, moreover, similarly, too
Contrast	although, but, however, in spite of, instead, nevertheless, on the other hand, otherwise, still, yet

Directions: Read the passage below and underline all the transition words and phrases you can find.

After dinner, we sang songs around the campfire and told stories. As the cool night air arrived, I pulled out my sleeping bag and unrolled it. Then Jeb and I took the pails down to the stream and filled them. We set them beside the fire and waited. Meanwhile everyone seemed to be dozing off. When I was certain that everyone was asleep, I used the water in the bucket to douse the fire. The hot logs sizzled as a result of being splashed with cold water.

Then I climbed into my sleeping bag and looked at the stars above me. Although I had spent a lot of time in the country, I had trouble remembering the formal names of the constellations. My father had tried to teach me, but I forgot. So I invented my own names, and I remembered them, too. Eventually I fell asleep and dreamed I could float in the sky like the stars.

The next morning, the first thing I did was restart the fire again. I knew the campers would never forgive me if they had to wait for their breakfasts. More important, I did not want to wait long for my first cup of coffee. Otherwise I would be very grumpy.

Identify five transition words or phrases in the passage. Explain how the transitions connect ideas. Write your explanations on a separate sheet of paper.

Copyright © 2007 by Holt, Rinehart and Winston. All rights reserved.

Type of Writing: Expository, Persuasive, or Narrative

Paragraphing

Directions: Read the paragraph below. Decide where the paragraph should be divided into three paragraphs. Draw a slash mark (/) to indicate where the breaks should occur. On the lines at the bottom of the page, explain why you started the new paragraphs where you did.

I have heard people talking about the proposed youth recreation center, and I believe that it is a fine idea. While some adults may think homework and chores are enough to keep students busy after school, there are still a few hours each afternoon when many of us are bored and restless. The youth center would take care of our needs to find safe, fun things to do. Those who don't agree with the plans for the center seem to think that young people always have another kid or two to do things with in our free time. That is not always the case. Since students have different schedules during the weekday afternoons and weekends, it is not always possible to find someone who is free. Sometimes I am actually lonely after school but don't want to just walk around downtown. There are people there who could get me into trouble. I want to avoid that type of crowd and find a safe place to hang out. My parents both have full-time jobs and would be glad if there were a youth center I could go to after school. Finally, I believe that there is a lot I can learn from the youth center programs. I have heard that such programs can offer games, singing groups, arts and crafts activities, and job counseling for older kids. These centers are also good places to make friends.

_____

_____

_____

_____

_____

_____

_____

_____

_____

_____

_____

Copyright © 2007 by Holt, Rinehart and Winston. All rights reserved.

SIX TRAITS: CONVENTIONS

Type of Writing: Expository, Persuasive, or Narrative

Usage: Verb Agreement and Verb Tense
Directions: Underline the subject of each sentence and the italicized verb in parentheses that agrees with the subject.

1. My sisters never (*enjoy, enjoys*) ice skating anymore.

2. The club members (*is, are*) planning an overnight hike.

3. No one but Jacqueline (*want, wants*) to go.

4. The local newspaper (*doesn't, don't*) print much foreign news.

5. Anybody who is interested in boats (*need, needs*) how to swim.

6. Neither of my grandmothers (*has, have*) retired.

7. Few of the documents (*was, were*) authentic.

8. Not one of the astronomers (*know, knows*) whether life exists on Mars.

9. Among writers, some (*has, have*) made predictions that came true.

10. A fleet of ships (*are, is*) sailing into the harbor.

11. Deneice and Maria (*play, plays*) volleyball after school.

12. Neither Ellie nor Noah (*read, reads*) much science fiction.

13. Ms. Galinsky or Mr. Wilson (*have, has*) the details about the meeting.

14. Would the committee please (*check, checks*) the date for the next meeting?

15. (*Don't, Doesn't*) the falling rain sound beautiful?

Directions: In the following paragraph, the verb tenses are not consistent. Decide whether the paragraph should be in the present or the past tense. Then on a separate sheet of paper, rewrite the paragraph, making sure to use consistent tense.

[11] Eleanor Roosevelt's parents died when she was a child, so she is raised by her grandmother and sent to school in England. [12] There she fell under the influenced of headmistress Marie Souvestre, who works for social causes. [13] As a young adult, Roosevelt participated in social work before she marries Franklin Delano Roosevelt. [14] After her husband enters politics, she works for the American Red Cross during World War I and later became more involved in politics herself. [15] In the early 1930s, Mrs. Roosevelt becomes a leading activist for women's rights. [16] When her husband was elected President of the United States, Mrs. Roosevelt helps other women get appointed to government positions. [17] She travels around the country, visited coal mines and slums, and speaks out for the poor. [18] After her husband's death, Mrs. Roosevelt is appointed by President Truman to be a delegate to the United Nations. [19] Her service to the U.N. is probably her greatest achievement. [20] Roosevelt devoted her whole life to causes of humanity and is loved by many.

Copyright © 2007 by Holt, Rinehart and Winston. All rights reserved.

SIX TRAITS: CONVENTIONS

Type of Writing: Expository, Persuasive, or Narrative

Standard Usage
Directions: Underline the word or expression in parentheses that is correct according to the standards for formal usage.

1. More people could *(have, of)* gone to the game if it hadn't rained.

2. That perfume smells really *(bad, badly)*.

3. No one really knows the *(affects, effects)* the new discovery will have.

4. There is *(fewer, less)* water in the local lakes because of the drought.

5. Tasha, why did you give *(them, those)* sweaters away?

6. We are fortunate to be able to *(choose, chose)* which classes to take.

7. Did you read *(that, where)* the pool will close early on Saturday?

8. Dad and I will *(try and, try to)* pull up all the weeds today.

9. We noticed that the twins helped *(theirselves, themselves)* to extra helpings.

10. When Nora is sad, she becomes *(real, very)* quiet.

11. The company report concludes that there *(ain't, isn't)* much demand for wigs.

12. Probably everyone *(accept, except)* Eliza is hoping for more snow.

13. Did Aaron tell you *(how come, why)* he didn't go to practice?

14. Sheryl's backpack zipper *(broke, busted)* as she walked to school.

15. The chores were divided equally *(among, between)* the three children.

16. The plant wilted in the sun and still does not look *(good, well)*.

17. *(A, An)* gila monster, a type of of desert lizard, isn't actually a monster.

18. The reason we have no e-mail is *(because, that)* the server is down.

19. Gretchen talked *(as if, like)* she wanted to the go the beach with us tomorrow.

20. In our school, country music is more popular *(than, then)* classical music.

21. *(Advertisers, Advertisers they)* often use exaggeration in their commercials.

22. Lola is not sure where Grafton Street *(is, is at)*.

23. Ms. Brown tried to *(learn, teach)* the eighth-graders about prime numbers.

24. To our astonishment, the ball landed *(outside, outside of)* the lines.

25. After the repair, the car's performance improved *(some, somewhat)*.

Copyright © 2007 by Holt, Rinehart and Winston. All rights reserved.

SIX TRAITS: CONVENTIONS

Type of Writing: Expository, Persuasive, or Narrative

Capitalization and Spelling

Directions: Circle the letters that should be capitalized in the following paragraph. Draw a slash through capital letters that should be lowercase.

America's food has been influenced by many Cultures. Who has not enjoyed chinese Egg drop soup, italian pasta, mexican tacos, or the german and scandinavian Cheeses from wisconsin. The smorgasbord may seem american, but the idea originated in sweden. Pretzels were originally dutch delicacies. Shish Kebab, which is often served at backyard Barbecues, is actually a turkish dish. No thanksgiving dinner would be complete without Turkey, corn, and pumpkin. These foods are truly American, for they were here long before the Pilgrims reached north America.

Directions: The following paragraph contains fifteen spelling errors. For each sentence, draw a line through any misspelled words and write the correct spelling above it.

[1] The Regional Art Club includes members from middle schools in twenty-two citys. [2] Art critics throughout the state conceed that our members are extremely talented. [3] "Use your imagination" and "Express your creativeity" are our mottos. [4] We have large studioes at four centrally located schools. [5] There is a large vareity of artistic stiles among our members. [6] Some students make huge sculpturs out of mettal objects. [7] The club is overun with painters, as you might expect. [8] Potters eassly come in secund in number. [9] Photogaphy is also a poplar art, especially with many students in the nineth grade. [10] Members usually meet once during the week and agin on Saturdays.

Copyright © 2007 by Holt, Rinehart and Winston. All rights reserved.

SIX TRAITS: CONVENTIONS

Type of Writing: Expository, Persuasive, or Narrative

Punctuation

Directions: Read the passage below and add commas, semicolons, colons, and end marks where they are needed.

One hundred years ago there were a hundred thousand elephants living in Asia however, now there are only about one third of that number What an alarming loss The Asian elephant is now an endangered species for the following reasons cutting of forests other damage to habitat and increased human population Of the Asian elephants that remain about ten thousand live in the small country of Myanmar Can you find the country in the atlas It is located between Thailand and Bangladesh Many of the huge patient elephants also called timber elephants work with humans together they bring in large valuable trees to sell for lumber Elephants and people have a partnership and they spend their lives together This partnership is remarkable for the mutual affection and trust it demonstrates between animals and humans

Directions: Read the passage below. Cross out any incorrect punctuation, and add any punctuation marks that have been omitted.

I propose that the group take a canoe trip down the Delaware said Nicky with enthusiasm! We could rent canoes in Callicoon and paddle down to Bingham Falls. I think that is a good idea Charlotte replied but how do we get the canoes back to Callicoon. Thats easy Nicky answered because there is a series of posts along the river where we can leave the canoes. We rent them at one post and check them at a post farther down the River. Lets schedule the trip for next weekend Bryce exclaimed.

Copyright © 2007 by Holt, Rinehart and Winston. All rights reserved.

SIX TRAITS: CONVENTIONS

Type of Writing: Expository, Persuasive, or Narrative

Proofreading: Checklist and Chart

Directions: Proofreading your own writing means checking it for mistakes in grammar, usage, spelling, capitalization, and punctuation. Use the following guidelines to help you review either your own or another student's writing. Then, use the chart below to record any errors that you find.

1. Is every sentence complete?

2. Does every sentence begin with a capital letter? Are proper nouns capitalized?

3. Does every sentence end with the correct punctuation mark?

4. Do subjects and verbs agree?

5. Are verbs in the right form and tense?

6. Are adjectives and adverb forms used correctly in making comparisons?

7. Are the forms of personal pronouns used correctly?

8. Does every pronoun agree with its antecedent (the word it refers to) in number and gender? Are pronoun references clear?

9. Are all words spelled correctly?

10. Is the writing neat and legible?

Error Log

Grammar and Usage	
Description of Problem	Location (Page and Line)

Spelling	
Misspelled Words	Correct Spellings

Capitalization	
Words with Errors	Corrections

Punctuation	
Description of Problem(s)	Location (Page and Line)

Copyright © 2007 by Holt, Rinehart and Winston. All rights reserved.

ANSWER KEY

On the next three pages you will find three completed evaluation forms for the practice essays that appear on pp. 33–34, 35–36, and 37–39. Use the scores on these evaluations to gauge students' own evaluating skills.

Completed Evaluation Chart for Expository Essay (pp. 33–34)

Scores	
Ideas and Content	3
Organization	4
Voice	4
Word Choice	3
Sentence Fluency	3
Conventions	5

Comments:

Ideas and Content: The writer has a solid and clear interpretation of the quotation in the writing prompt. He or she makes two clear connections between wars and earthquakes. The paper is short, however, and does not explore the topic thoroughly.

Organization: The organization is clear. The writer discusses two ways in which wars and earthquakes are alike.

Voice: The writer's concern about the impact of war and earthquake is clear. Readers can sense the writer's personal feelings but are not deeply engaged.

Word Choice: The writer's word choices are adequate. They convey her feelings and ideas, but they do not sparkle much.

Sentence Fluency: The writer does have some sentence variety in terms of mixing sentence lengths and sentence with varied beginnings. He or she also uses transitional words and phrases consistently, but the paper is too short, and the sentences lack rhythm or style.

Conventions: The writer has a firm and consistent grasp of writing conventions.

Sum It Up: Overall I thought the paper was written with conviction and shows a good grasp of the impact of wars and earthquakes. The writer clearly felt strongly about his or her ideas but could have written much more and made deeper connections. The paper is adequate but could have been longer and made more comparisons and contrasts.

Copyright © 2007 by Holt, Rinehart and Winston. All rights reserved.

Completed Evaluation Chart for Persuasive Essay (pp. 35–37)

Scores	
Ideas and Content	1
Organization	1
Voice	1
Word Choice	1
Sentence Fluency	1
Conventions	1

Comments:

Ideas and Content: The writer repeats the prompt questions in the introduction without adding any original ideas, which indicates he or she has no opinion or thoughts to share. The phrase "Some say yes, some say no" indicates that the writer will not take a stand, offering instead a wishy-washy response. The reasons the writer provides are not well thought out, nor are they articulated well. The details are random and often unrelated. For example, the colors of the Bruins' football uniforms are completely unrelated to the topic and distracting.

Organization: The paper has no clear sense of organization. It meanders from one under-developed point to the next.

Voice: The voice cannot be established because the writer has no point of view or opinion about the topic. The voice conveys neither personality nor feeling.

Word Choice: The writer's choice of words is limited, repetitive, and uninteresting.

Sentence Fluency: The paper contains sentence fragments and poorly constructed sentences. Transitions are barely used to show connections between ideas and sentences. The sentences show no style.

Conventions: The paper is riddled with errors in punctuation, spelling, and grammar and usage.

Sum It Up: Overall I thought the paper was probably written quickly and without any original thought. The writer makes no attempt to offer any ideas or analysis. His or her reasons and evidence seem randomly selected. The language is barely adequate and repetitive. It conveys nothing about the writer's personality or thinking processes. The writer clearly needs to brush up on the conventions of writing.

Copyright © 2007 by Holt, Rinehart and Winston. All rights reserved.

Completed Evaluation Chart for Narrative Essay (pp. 37–39)

Scores	
Ideas and Content	5
Organization	5
Voice	5
Word Choice	5
Sentence Fluency	5
Conventions	5

Comments:

Ideas and Content: The writer tells an original story that conveys a lesson she has learned. The story is original and interesting and filled with details that appeal to the senses.

Organization: The narrative tells events in the order they occurred and uses pacing to build suspense.

Voice: The writer's voice is really apparent here. Through dialogue, inner monologue, and details, the writer reveals her original thoughts and feelings during the experience. The voice really engages the reader.

Word Choice: The writer chooses words carefully, and she successfully conveys the experience. Her language appeals to the senses, and her dialogue sounds realistic and fresh.

Sentence Fluency: The sentences are varied and well constructed and often sophisticated. They contain transitions that help readers follow the course of events in the story. The sentences flow so nicely that readers are not distracted. They can pay attention to the events of the story.

Conventions: The writer has a clear and consistent grasp of writing conventions.

Sum It Up: Overall I thought the paper was excellent. The writer obviously enjoyed writing it. Her writing is vivid and interesting, and her voice is lively. The writer clearly learned something from her uncle and wanted to share her experience with others. Well done!

p. 97 Identifying Tone

Possible responses:

Passage 1: Possible tones: formal, whiny, slightly unreasonable

Reason: The writer sounds like he or she is complaining by focusing on the unfairness. He or she repeats the word "unfair" several times and uses qualifying phrases such as "one bit of credit," "really unfair," and "plain unfair."

Passage 2: Possible tones: informal, conversational, disrespectful

Reason: The tone sounds like someone speaking—like one teen speaking to another. The writer uses slang and disrespectful terms, such as "Duh!" and "Whatever."

Passage 3: Possible tones: reasonable, formal, thoughtful

Reason: The writer sounds as though he or she respects the audience and cares about the topic. He or she uses "we" as well as formal language.

Copyright © 2007 by Holt, Rinehart and Winston. All rights reserved.

p. 98 Recognizing Connotations

Possible responses:

1. *naughty* **Definition:** not behaved; **Connotation:** When you are naughty, you are mischievous in a cute kind of way.

2. *challenging* **Definition:** difficult, hard; **Connotation:** *Challenging* means "difficult in a way that makes a person stretch or try to improve him or herself."

3. *oozed* **Definition:** flowed or leaked; **Connotation:** Here the word sounds like a leak that is disgusting or yucky.

4. *recognition* **Definition:** acknowledgement; **Connotation**: *Recognition* means "not only being seen but also being given approval."

5. *sensitive* **Definition:** easily affected; **Connotation:** The word suggests that the person is too easily affected and is actually kind of annoying.

page 99 Avoiding Loaded Language, Jargon, and Clichés

1. **C** cat out of the bag
2. **LL** honest, hardworking Americans
3. **J** the numbers
4. **C** pretty as a picture
5. **C** red as a lobster
6. **J** Wall Street, the Dow and NASDAQ
7. **J** log on, password, PIN
8. **LL** quacks
9. **C** mad as a wet hen
10. **LL** incompetent bureaucrat, waste
11. **J** scan, bar code
12. **C** flat as a pancake
13. **C** great, very unique
14. **LL** fat cat politicians
15. **LL** wannabes and posers

page 100 Avoiding Passive Voice

PV 1. Sharmaine served the tennis ball.

AV 2. no correction needed

PV 3. Several new people attended the class.

PV 4. Many tourists viewed the art in the museum.

PV 5. The tree trimmer pruned our pecan tree.

PV 6. The veterinarian gave the dog its rabies vaccination.

PV 7. The technician fixed the computer.

AV 8. no correction needed

AV 9. no correction needed

Below is the paragraph with its "to be" verbs underlined. The corrected version follows.

[1] The arctic tundra <u>is characterized</u> by long winters, little snow, and low temperatures. [2] Warm summer temperatures thaw the tundra's surface soil but not the subsoil, or permafrost. [3] Therefore, drainage <u>is hindered</u> by flat and partially frozen ground. [4] Ponds and bogs <u>are formed</u> by standing water. [5] Typical artic vegetation includes low plants, such as cotton grass, sedge, and lichens. [6] Soil disturbances such as "flowing soil" <u>are caused</u> by thaws and movement of soil. [7] Irregular landforms, such as hummocks, frost boils, and earth stripes, <u>are produced</u> by poorly drained areas. [8] On the soft surface, deep gullies <u>are caused</u> by vehicle tracks. [9] Most arctic vegetation can survive these soil disturbances. [10] Likewise, arctic wildlife <u>is</u> also not deeply <u>affected</u> by these changes.

[1] Long winters, little snow, and low temperatures characterize the arctic tundra. [2] Warm summer temperatures thaw the tundra's surface soil but not the subsoil, or permafrost. [3] Therefore, flat and partially frozen ground hinders drainage. [4] Standing water forms ponds and bogs. [5] Typical artic vegeta-

Copyright © 2007 by Holt, Rinehart and Winston. All rights reserved.

tion includes low plants, such as cotton grass, sedge, and lichens. [6] Thaws and movement of soil cause soil disturbances such as "flowing soil." [7] Poorly drained areas form irregular landforms, such as hummocks, frost boils, and earth stripes. [8] On the soft surface, vehicle tracks form deep gullies. [9] Most arctic vegetation can survive these soil disturbances. [10] These changes do not deeply affect arctic wildlife either.

page 101 Revising for Sentence Variety
Possible revision:

The Populist movement was an American movement that developed in the 1800s. It began during the depression of the late 1870s when farmers were losing money then. They formed organized groups called Farmers' Alliances. Members of the alliances worked together. They built barns for storing the crops, which stayed in the barns until the prices were better. Some alliances included African American farmers. Although African American farmers could not vote, the alliances welcomed them anyway.

The alliances became powerful at the end of the century and formed a national political party. They joined forces with another group called the Knights of Labor. The two groups formed the People's Party, and its members were known as Populists. Populists wanted the national government to change. They wanted it to print more paper money because more paper money might raise farm prices. The Populists also wanted a national income tax. Americans did not pay income tax then. Although it was not a popular idea, it became a reality when Congress passed the sixteenth amendment in 1913, which made a national income tax legal. Americans have paid income tax ever since.

page 102 Revising Run-on Sentences
The revised passage should appear as follows:

Today when modern meteorologists forecast the weather, they can count on the help of an impressive battery of scientific devices. Weather satellites, for example, relay photographs of cloud formations from all over the world. These pictures show where storms are beginning over oceans and deserts. The paths of typhoons and hurricanes are tracked the same way. Weather information from all sources is fed into powerful computers. Thus the weather can be evaluated with amazing speed.

Our ancestors had no complicated weather instruments. They had to rely on their eyes and ears and a few old proverbs and maxims. Their methods were hardly scientific. Today, for example, no one still believes the old superstition about the groundhog, but we celebrate Groundhog Day just the same. The story goes that if the groundhog sees its shadow on the second day of February, there will be six more months of winter. Watch for yourself and see! The behavior of insects, on the other hand, is still a good indicator of temperature because they are cold blooded. Grasshoppers cannot fly when the temperature drops below 55 degrees Fahrenheit. If you hear a cricket chirping, count the number of chirps in fourteen seconds and add forty. Then you will have the temperature in degrees Fahrenheit.

Today weather forecasting is much more accurate if less charming than it was in the old days. However, the forecasters are still not always right, perhaps because there are so many factors to consider.

Copyright © 2007 by Holt, Rinehart and Winston. All rights reserved.

page 103 Revising Stringy and Wordy Sentences

Possible revision:

Argentina is a country in South America. It borders the south Atlantic, and its capital is Buenos Aires. My friend Leela has been to Argentina. She went with her family while her father studied at a university there. Leela had a great time meeting people, and she got to speak in Spanish. Leela spent time in the city, but she also went to the countryside where she learned about the life of the cowboys of South America. She was very impressed, so she wrote a story about her experiences. It is about a character named Tanmoor. He is an interesting character even though he is from a small town in Argentina. However, he wants to move to the big city. The story has an interesting beginning. It opens with Tanmoor's father working on a ranch. He is a *vaquero*—a cowboy, and the bank wants to put him out of business. Tanmoor is trying to help save the ranch. Leela clearly did lots of research and asked a lot of questions. It shows because the story is excellent!

Possible revision:

When the daughters of pioneers were young girls, they learned how to sew and cook. Young girls had to learn household skills because otherwise the chores wouldn't get done. So girls would carefully and thoughtfully attend their mother's instructions. They had to do all sorts of chores that we don't even do anymore, like make butter, bake bread, and wash clothes by hand. Today we have convenient machines to do household chores. In addition, we never have to cook because we can go to the grocery store and buy any ready-to-eat food we want. Life was hard for pioneer women, and we should be grateful that we can get many jobs done with a flip of a switch.

page 104 Choppy Sentences and Sentence Combining

1. The Himalayas are the tallest mountains in Asia.
2. Tea bushes grow on steep slopes on the fertile hills near Darjeeling.
3. The great danger in climbing comes from the high altitude and the bitter cold.
4. Marissa and Mara will hike in Rocky Mountain National Park and pitch tents in Hidden Valley.
5. Marissa and Mara have their own camping equipment and they both know how to use it.
6. The two young women love camping and hiking.
7. Alexander the Great's father was the king of Macedonia.
8. Alexander wanted to tame a horse that was afraid of its own shadow.
9. Alexander turned the horse around so it faced the sun and could not see its own shadow, and it calmed down.
10. This story is an example of how Alexander the Great tamed the wild horse with kindness and compassion.

page 105 Using Transitional Words and Phrases

The transitional words and phrases are underlined.

<u>After</u> dinner, we sang songs <u>around</u> the campfire <u>and</u> told stories. <u>As the</u> cool night air arrived, I pulled out my sleeping bag <u>and</u> unrolled it. <u>Then</u> Jeb <u>and</u> I took the pails <u>down</u> to the stream <u>and</u> filled them. We set them <u>beside</u> the fire <u>and</u> waited. <u>Meanwhile</u> everyone seemed to be dozing off. <u>When</u> I was certain that

Copyright © 2007 by Holt, Rinehart and Winston. All rights reserved.

everyone was asleep, I used the water <u>in</u> the bucket to douse the fire. The hot logs sizzled <u>as a result of</u> being splashed with cold water.

    <u>Then</u> I climbed <u>into</u> my sleeping bag <u>and</u> looked at the stars <u>above</u> me. <u>Although</u> I had spent a lot of time <u>in</u> the country, I had trouble remembering the formal names of the constellations. My father had tried to teach me, <u>but</u> I forgot. <u>So</u> I invented my own names, <u>and</u> I remembered them, <u>too</u>. <u>Eventually</u> I fell asleep <u>and</u> dreamed I could float <u>in</u> the sky <u>like</u> the stars.

    The <u>next</u> morning, the <u>first</u> thing I did was restart the fire again. I knew the campers would never forgive me if they had to wait for their breakfasts. <u>More important,</u> I did not want to wait long for my first cup of coffee. <u>Otherwise</u> I would be very grumpy.

page 106 Paragraphing

The first paragraph should end after "fun things to do." The second paragraph should begin "Those who don't agree" and end with "I could go to after school." The third paragraph should begin with "Finally, I believe." Students should understand that the paragraph breaks occur when the writer identifies and explains a new point.

page 107 Verb Agreement and Verb Tense

1. enjoy	**4.** doesn't	**7.** were	**10.** is	**13.** has
2. are	**5.** needs	**8.** knows	**11.** play	**14.** check
3. wants	**6.** has	**9.** have	**12.** reads	**15.** Doesn't

The following revised paragraph uses verbs in the past tense:

    [11] Eleanor Roosevelt's parents died when she was a child, so she was raised by her grandmother and sent to school in England. [12] There she fell under the influence of headmistress Marie Souvestre, who worked for social causes. [13] As a young adult, Roosevelt participated in social work before she married Franklin Delano Roosevelt. [14] After her husband entered politics, she worked for the American Red Cross during World War I and later became more involved in politics herself. [15] In the early 1930s, Mrs. Roosevelt became a leading activist for women's rights. [16] When her husband was elected President of the United States, Mrs. Roosevelt helped other women get appointed to government positions. [17] She traveled around the country, visited coal mines and slums, and spoke out for the poor. [18] After her husband's death, Mrs. Roosevelt was appointed by President Truman to be a delegate to the United Nations. [19] Her service to the U.N. was probably her greatest achievement. [20] Roosevelt devoted her whole life to causes of humanity and was loved by many.

page 108 Standard Usage

1. have	**6.** choose	**11.** isn't	**16.** good	**21.** Advertisers
2. bad	**7.** that	**12.** except	**17.** A	**22.** is
3. effects	**8.** try to	**13.** why	**18.** that	**23.** teach
4. less	**9.** themselves	**14.** broke	**19.** as if	**24.** outside
5. those	**10.** very	**15.** among	**20.** than	**25.** somewhat

Copyright © 2007 by Holt, Rinehart and Winston. All rights reserved.

page 109 Capitalization and Spelling Corrected passage (corrected words are underlined):

America's food has been influenced by many <u>cultures</u>. Who has not enjoyed <u>Chinese egg</u> drop soup, <u>Italian</u> pasta, <u>Mexican</u> tacos, or the <u>German</u> and <u>Scandinavian cheeses</u> from <u>Wisconsin</u>. The smorgasbord may seem <u>American</u>, but the idea originated in <u>Sweden</u>. Pretzels were originally <u>Dutch</u> delicacies. Shish Kebab, which is often served at backyard <u>barbecues</u>, is actually a <u>Turkish</u> dish. No thanksgiving dinner would be complete without <u>turkey</u>, corn, and pumpkin. These foods are truly American, for they were here long before the <u>pilgrims</u> reached <u>North</u> America.

Corrected passage (corrected words are underlined):

[1] The Regional Art Club includes members from middle schools in twenty-two <u>cities</u>. [2] Art critics throughout the state <u>concede</u> that our members are extremely talented. [3] "Use your imagination" and "Express your <u>creativity</u>" are our mottos. [4] We have large <u>studios</u> at four centrally located schools. [5] There is a large <u>variety</u> of artistic <u>styles</u> among our members. [6] Some students make huge <u>sculptures</u> out of <u>metal</u> objects. [7] The club is <u>overrun</u> with painters, as you might expect. [8] Potters <u>easily</u> come in <u>second</u> in number. [9] <u>Photography</u> is also a <u>popular</u> art, especially with many students in the <u>ninth</u> grade. [10] Members usually meet once during the week and <u>again</u> on Saturdays.

page 111 Punctuation Corrected passage (corrections are underlined):

One hundred years ago<u>,</u> there were a hundred thousand elephants living in Asia<u>;</u> however, now there are only about one third of that number<u>.</u> What an alarming loss! The Asian elephant is now an endangered species for the following reasons: cutting of forests<u>,</u> other damage to habitat<u>,</u> and increased human population<u>.</u> Of the Asian elephants that remain<u>,</u> about ten thousand live in the small country of Myanmar<u>.</u> Can you find the country in the atlas<u>?</u> It is located between Thailand and Bangladesh<u>.</u> Many of the huge<u>,</u> patient elephants<u>,</u> also called timber elephants<u>,</u> work with humans<u>;</u> together they bring in large valuable trees to sell for lumber<u>.</u> Elephants and people have a partnership<u>,</u> and they spend their lives together<u>.</u> This partnership is remarkable for the mutual affection and trust it demonstrates between animals and humans<u>.</u>

Corrected passage (corrections are underlined):

<u>"</u>I propose that the group take a canoe trip down the Delaware<u>!"</u> said Nicky with enthusiasm<u>. "</u>We could rent canoes in Callicoon and paddle down to Bingham Falls<u>." "</u>I think that is a good idea<u>,"</u> Charlotte replied<u>, "</u>but how do we get the canoes back to Callicoon<u>?" "</u>That's easy<u>,"</u> Nicky answered<u>, "</u>because there is a series of posts along the river where we can leave the canoes. We rent them at one post and check them at a post farther down the River<u>." "</u>Let's schedule the trip for next weekend<u>!"</u> Bryce exclaimed.

Copyright © 2007 by Holt, Rinehart and Winston. All rights reserved.